PRAISE FOR
SNOW WHITE LEARNS WITCHCRAFT

"This lush collection artfully gathers together many of World Fantasy Award winner Goss's fairy tale–themed poems and short fiction published over the last 16 years, including her Locus-nominated story 'Red as Blood and White as Bone.' As a Hungarian-American raised on Hans Christen Andersen and the Brothers Grimm, Goss takes obvious delight in reweaving classic European folk tales to reveal new, often deeply feminist, perspectives. In 'The Gold-Spinner,' Rumpelstiltskin is recast as a girl lying to save herself, while 'Conversations with the Sea Witch' features the Little Mermaid as an old woman looking back on a life both difficult and well-lived. In 'A Country Called Winter,' a college student must come to terms with her birthright as ice threatens to overtake the world, while 'Mr. Fox' explores the balance of power between lovers, and the choice to say no to a future others have laid out is celebrated in 'The Princess and the Frog.' Perhaps most poignant of all, 'The Nightingale and the Rose' is a beautiful, sensitive reminder that storybook love is not all it's cracked up to be. This toothsome collection is best read in one go."

—*Publishers Weekly,* **starred review**

"Theodora Goss re-fleshes and re-clothes old tales in multifarious ways. Sometimes the stories' new garments are classic and mythic, sometimes they're up-to-the-minute, twenty-first-century creations, fresh cuts and colors that bring new truths from the underlying structures. Through prose and poetry, Goss shines her unique light into the fairytale forest—and many bright eyes gleam back."

—**Margo Lanagan,** *New York Times*–**bestselling and World Fantasy Award–winning author of** *Tender Morsels*

"I was expecting this to be good, but it's wonderful. Seeing these pieces together makes me realize what a vivid, authentic and important voice Goss is. These are real fairytales, magical, unsettling, touching, and brilliant. I loved every word."

—**Jo Walton, World Fantasy, Nebula, and Hugo award–winning author of** *Among Others*

"Theodora Goss's *Snow White Learns Witchcraft* is a gorgeous, lyric collection of fairy tale retellings. Goss has the ability—the witchcraft—to be able to see the heart of the tale, and show it, polished and reflected and new, to the reader. I loved these stories and poems, their wildness, their beauty, their truth."

—**Kat Howard, Alex Award–winning author**
of *An Unkindness of Magicians*

"With each story, Theodora Goss weaves new myths from the threads of childhood and legend. This collection does what the best songs and poems and spells do: slips gently into your consciousness, then slowly changes the way you see the world. A wonderful addition to Goss's works."

—**Fran Wilde, World Fantasy, Nebula, and Hugo finalist and author of the award-winning Bone Universe trilogy**

"The elegance of Goss's work has never ceased to amaze me. It feels effortless, but endlessly evocative and suggestive, flowing with the rhythms of both the natural world and the intimate socio-familial cosmos. Goss's language fits together like gems in a complex crown, a diadem of images and motifs, resting gently on the head, but with a deceptive weight."

—**Catherynne M. Valente,** *New York Times*–
bestselling author of *Space Opera*

"In *Snow White Learns Witchcraft*, Theodora Goss weaves words that look disturbingly like snow and feathers into new stories that are familiar but uniquely remade. A Goss heroine breathes life into silent castles, imprints her own image in darkling mirrors, and plucks enchanted apples from the hands of peddlers; she is a bear's bride, a newly minted queen, a thunderstorm of a woman and so much more. Dr. Goss cements her position as one of our foremost re-interpreters of fairy tales."

—**Angela Slatter, World Fantasy Award–**
winning author of *The Bitterwood Bible*

"What will you find in these pages, dear reader? Why, the encyclopedia of everything (as written by an owl), what the mirror really knows, rubies red with wolf's blood—and, surprise!—the secret of who actually spun that straw into gold. Ice, iron, apples, birds, bones, subversion: Theodora Goss's new collection of stories and poems *Snow White Learns Witchcraft* is woven of the finest spider silk, a funnel-web of faerie tales that will catch you fast and not let you go."

—**C. S. E. Cooney, World Fantasy Award–**
winning author of *Bone Swans*

Snow White Learns Witchcraft

Also by Theodora Goss

Novels

The Extraordinary Adventures of the Athena Club
THE STRANGE CASE OF THE ALCHEMIST'S DAUGHTER
EUROPEAN TRAVEL FOR THE MONSTROUS GENTLEWOMAN
THE SINISTER MYSTERY OF THE MESMERIZING GIRL (forthcoming)

Novellas

THE THORN AND THE BLOSSOM

Short Fiction Collections

IN THE FOREST OF FORGETTING
THE ROSE IN TWELVE PETALS & OTHER STORIES

Poetry Collections

SONGS FOR OPHELIA

As Editor

INTERFICTIONS: An Anthology of Interstitial Writing
(with Delia Sherman)

VOICES FROM FAIRYLAND:
The Fantastical Poems of Mary Coleridge,
Charlotte Mew, and Sylvia Townsend Warner

SNOW WHITE LEARNS WITCHCRAFT

STORIES AND POEMS

THEODORA GOSS

INTRODUCTION BY JANE YOLEN

Mythic Delirium
BOOKS

mythicdelirium.com

Snow White Learns Witchcraft
Stories and Poems

FIRST EDITION
February 5, 2019

ISBN-10: 1-7326440-0-4
ISBN-13: 978-1-7326440-0-7

Library of Congress Control Number: 2018960573

Published by Mythic Delirium Books
mythicdelirium.com

Further copyright information begins on page 220.

Our gratitude goes out to the following who because of their generosity are from now on designated as supporters of Mythic Delirium Books: Saira Ali, Cora Anderson, Anonymous, Patricia M. Cryan, Steve Dempsey, Oz Drummond, Patrick Dugan, Matthew Farrer, C. R. Fowler, Mary J. Lewis, Paul T. Muse, Jr., Shyam Nunley, Finny Pendragon, Kenneth Schneyer, and Delia Sherman.

For Terri Windling, Queen of Faerie

Contents

A Welcome to the Coven: Introduction by Jane Yolen 11

Snow White Learns Witchcraft 13

The Ogress Queen 16

The Rose in Twelve Petals 18

Thorns and Briars 35

Rose Child 37

Thumbelina 41

Blanchefleur 42

Mr. Fox 82

What Her Mother Said 84

Snow, Blood, Fur 86

The Red Shoes 90

Girl, Wolf, Woods 92

Red as Blood and White as Bone 94

The Gold-Spinner 116

Rumpelstiltskin 118

Goldilocks and the Bear 120

Sleeping With Bears 124

The Stepsister's Tale 131

The Clever Serving-Maid 133

Seven Shoes 135

The Other Thea 138

The Sensitive Woman 165

The Bear's Wife 166

The Bear's Daughter 168

A Country Called Winter 169

How to Make It Snow 189

Diamonds and Toads 194

The Princess and the Frog 197

Conversations with the Sea Witch 199

The Nightingale and the Rose 207

Mirror, Mirror 215

A Welcome to the Coven

Jane Yolen

I have known Theodora (Dora) Goss for a number of years but in the shorthand way we busy writers get to know each other—reading one another's blogs or Facebook pages, spending quick time at conferences, on panels together, the occasional email. Sometimes we even get to read one another's books—when we are not mired in research or writing our own.

I knew Dora was a Hungarian American born in Budapest, a college teacher, fiction writer, and poet. I knew her writing has been nominated for major awards, including the Nebula, Locus, Mythopoeic, and World Fantasy awards. But we never actually got to really sit down for the kind of days-on-end chats that you share with close friends, for she lives almost three hours away in Boston. She's a city mouse and I am a country mouse.

And honestly, the few times in the past years that I have gone to Boston, it was to see a granddaughter in graduate school, to sign at bookstores, to be *on* at Boskone, or visit one or two of my publishers there.

So I knew Dora enough to give her a hug whenever I saw her, to admire the poetry of hers that I'd read, to enjoy her on panels. Even to hear her read.

And then I was asked to write an introduction to her book of stories and poems. This book. *Snow White Learns Witchcraft.* My favorite topic—fairy tales fractured, reinvented, re-imagined, retold.

I am glad I said yes. No—*I am thrilled* I said yes. Here is the reason why: There are seven female fabulists whose work always blows me away—Isak Dinesen, Sylvia Townsend Warner, Angela Carter, Robin McKinley, Delia Sherman, Ellen Kushner, Terri Windling. They each bring charm, clarity, magic, exquisite writing, depth of fairy-tale/fantasy knowledge to their work, a constant inventiveness, and truth to their stories and poems. That's a devastating combination in any writer. But for the ones who deal in the folk tales and fairy tales of the past, absolutely crucial.

To this coven, I now add Theodora Goss. Her stories in this book are full of both folk and historical lore. She transposes, transforms, and transcends times, eras, and old tales with ease.

But also there is a core of tough magic that runs through all her pieces like a river through Faerie.

Here we have stories and poems that are and are not (or are more than) just Cinderella or Snow White or Red Riding Hood and other classics. They are those known tales totally made anew. In Dora's hands they have become something special, unforgettable, often set in a quasi Middle or East European setting in the 18th to 20th century that feels both invented and true.

All I can add is this: read this book—you will not be sorry. Or rather if you do *not* read it, you *will* be sorry. I am ready to reread some of my new favorites: "The Other Thea," full of shadows; the perfection of "The Rose in Twelve Petals"; the inventive twisting of the French fairy tale, *The White Cat* (one of my personal old favorites), into "Blanchefleur."

Rereading is not something I do with most stories. But the coven's work—*that*, I go back to again and again.

Welcome, Dora. It's about time you got here.

Snow White
Learns Witchcraft

One day she looked into her mother's mirror.
The face looking back was unavoidably old,
with wrinkles around the eyes and mouth. I've smiled
a lot, she thought. Laughed less, and cried a little.
A decent life, considered altogether.

She'd never asked it the fatal question that leads
to a murderous heart and red-hot iron shoes.
But now, being curious, when it scarcely mattered,
she recited *Mirror, mirror,* and asked the question:
Who is the fairest? Would it be her daughter?

No, the mirror told her. Some peasant girl
in a mountain village she'd never even heard of.

Well, let her be fairest. It wasn't so wonderful
being fairest. Sure, you got to marry the prince,
at least if you were royal, or become his mistress
if you weren't, because princes don't marry commoners,
whatever the stories tell you. It meant your mother,
whose skin was soft and smelled of parma violets,
who watched your father with a jealous eye,
might try to eat your heart, metaphorically—
or not. It meant the huntsman sent to kill you
would try to grab and kiss you before you ran
into the darkness of the sheltering forest.

How comfortable it was to live with dwarves
who didn't find her particularly attractive.
Seven brothers to whom she was just a child, and then,

once she grew tall, an ungainly adolescent,
unlike the shy, delicate dwarf women
who lived deep in the forest. She was constantly tripping
over the child-sized furniture they carved
with patterns of hearts and flowers on winter evenings.

She remembers when the peddler woman came
to her door with laces, a comb, and then an apple.
How pretty you are, my dear, the peddler told her.
It was the first time anyone had said
that she was pretty since she left the castle.
She didn't recognize her. And if she had?
Mother? She would have said. *Mother, is that you?*
How would her mother have answered? Sometimes she wishes
the prince had left her sleeping in the coffin.

He claimed he woke her up with true love's kiss.
The dwarves said actually his footman tripped
and jogged the apple out. She prefers that version.
It feels less burdensome, less like she owes him.

Because she never forgave him for the shoes,
red-hot iron, and her mother dancing in them,
the smell of burning flesh. She still has nightmares.
It wasn't supposed to be fatal, he insisted.
Just teach her a lesson. Give her blisters or boils,
make her repent her actions. No one dies
from dancing in iron shoes. She must have had
some sort of heart condition. And after all,
the woman did try to kill you. She didn't answer.

And so she inherited her mother's mirror,
but never consulted it, knowing too well
the price of coveting beauty. She watched her daughter
grow up, made sure the girl could run and fight,
because princesses need protecting, and sometimes princes
are worse than useless. When her husband died,
she went into mourning, secretly relieved
that it was over: a woman's useful life,

nurturing, procreative. Now, she thinks,
I'll go to the house by the seashore where in summer
we would take the children (really a small castle),
with maybe one servant. There, I will grow old,
wrinkled and whiskered. My hair as white as snow,
my lips thin and bloodless, my skin mottled.

I'll walk along the shore collecting shells,
read all the books I've never had the time for,
and study witchcraft. What should women do
when they grow old and useless? Become witches.
It's the only role you get to write yourself.

I'll learn the words to spells out of old books,
grow poisonous herbs and practice curdling milk,
cast evil eyes. I'll summon a familiar:
black cat or toad. I'll tell my grandchildren
fairy tales in which princesses slay dragons
or wicked fairies live happily ever after.
I'll talk to birds, and they'll talk back to me.
Or snakes—the snakes might be more interesting.

This is the way the story ends, she thinks.
It ends. And then you get to write your own story.

The Ogress Queen

I can smell him: little Helios.
He smells of cinnamon
and sugar. I can smell him even though
he is down in the garden, playing with a ball
and his dog, whom he calls Pantoufle.
"Here, Pantoufle," he cries. "Here, catch!"
I would like to catch him by the collar,
lick the back of his neck, suck up
the beads of sweat between his shoulder blades
(for it is a hot day, and there is no shade
in the castle garden except under the lime trees).
He would taste like brioche, oozing butter.
(Oh, his cheeks! so fat! so brown!
as though toasted.)
He would taste like sugar and cinnamon
and ginger.

And then little Aurora. She, I am convinced,
would taste of vanilla and almonds,
like marzipan. Less robust, more delicate
than her brother. I would save her for after.
Look, there she is in her white dress,
all frills and laces, like a doll
covered with royal icing,
rolling her hoop.
If I dipped her in water,
she would melt.

And walking along the path, I see
her mother, reading a book.

Love poems, no doubt—she is so sentimental.
She has kept every letter from my husband,
the king. She has kept,
somehow, her virtue intact, despite
the violation, despite the rude awakening
by two children she does not recall conceiving.
She resembles a galette:
rich, filled with succulent peaches
and frangipane. I will eat her
slowly, savoring her caramel hair,
her toes like raisins
dried from muscat grapes.
I will particularly enjoy
her eyes, which stare at me
with such limpid placidity,
as though she had not stolen my husband.
They will taste like candied citrons.

Today, today I will go talk to the cook
while the king is away at war
and order him to serve them up, one by one,
slice by slice, with perhaps
a glass of Riesling. Then at last my hunger
for my husband beside me in the bed at night,
for a son to rule after him while I am regent,
for warm, fragrant flesh,
spiced and smelling of cinnamon,
may be appeased.

The Rose in Twelve Petals

I. The Witch

This rose has twelve petals. Let the first one fall: Madeleine taps the glass bottle, and out tumbles a bit of pink silk that clinks on the table—a chip of tinted glass—no, look closer, a crystallized rose petal. She lifts it into a saucer and crushes it with the back of a spoon until it is reduced to lumpy powder and a puff of fragrance.

She looks at the book again. "Petal of one rose crushed, dung of small bat soaked in vinegar." Not enough light comes through the cottage's small-paned windows, and besides she is growing near-sighted, although she is only thirty-two. She leans closer to the page. He should have given her spectacles rather than pearls. She wrinkles her forehead to focus her eyes, which makes her look prematurely old, as in a few years she no doubt will be.

Bat dung has a dank, uncomfortable smell, like earth in caves that has never seen sunlight.

Can she trust it, this book? Two pounds ten shillings it cost her, including postage. She remembers the notice in *The Gentlewoman's Companion*: "Every lady her own magician. Confound your enemies, astonish your friends! As simple as a cookery manual." It looks magical enough, with *Compendium Magicarum* stamped on its spine and gilt pentagrams on its red leather cover. But the back pages advertise "a most miraculous lotion, that will make any lady's skin as smooth as an infant's bottom" and the collected works of Scott.

Not easy to spare ten shillings, not to mention two pounds, now that the King has cut off her income. Rather lucky, this cottage coming so cheap, although it has no proper plumbing, just a privy out back among the honeysuckle.

Madeleine crumbles a pair of dragonfly wings into the bowl, which is already half full: orris root; cat's bones found on the village dust heap; oak gall from a branch fallen into a fairy ring; madder, presumably for its color; crushed rose petal; bat dung.

And the magical words, are they quite correct? She knows a little Latin, learned from her brother. After her mother's death, when her father began spending days in his bedroom with a bottle of beer, she tended the shop, selling flour and printed cloth to the village women, scythes and tobacco to the men, sweets to children on their way to school. When her brother came home, he would sit at the counter beside her, saying his *amo, amas*. The silver cross he earned by taking a Hibernian bayonet in the throat is the only necklace she now wears.

She binds the mixture with water from a hollow stone and her own saliva. Not pleasant this, she was brought up not to spit, but she imagines she is spitting into the King's face, that first time when he came into the shop, and leaned on the counter, and smiled through his golden beard. "If I had known there was such a pretty shopkeeper in this village, I would have done my own shopping long ago."

She remembers: buttocks covered with golden hair among folds of white linen, like twin halves of a peach on a napkin. "Come here, Madeleine." The sounds of the palace, horses clopping, pageboys shouting to one another in the early morning air. "You'll never want for anything, haven't I told you that?" A string of pearls, each as large as her smallest fingernail, with a clasp of gold filigree. "Like it? That's Hibernian work, taken in the siege of London." Only later does she notice that between two pearls, the knotted silk is stained with blood.

She leaves the mixture under cheesecloth, to dry overnight.

Madeleine walks into the other room, the only other room of the cottage, and sits at the table that serves as her writing desk. She picks up a tin of throat lozenges. How it rattles. She knows, without opening it, that there are five pearls left, and that after next month's rent there will only be four.

Confound your enemies, she thinks, peering through the inadequate light, and the wrinkles on her forehead make her look prematurely old, as in a few years she certainly will be.

II. The Queen

Petals fall from the roses that hang over the stream, Empress Josephine and Gloire de Dijon, which dislike growing so close to the water. This corner of the garden has been planted to resemble a country landscape in miniature: artificial stream with ornamental fish, a pear tree that has never yet bloomed, bluebells that the gardener plants out every spring. This is the Queen's favorite part of the garden, although the roses dislike her as well, with her romantically diaphanous gowns, her lisping voice, her poetry.

Here she comes, reciting Tennyson.

She holds her arms out, allowing her sleeves to drift on the slight breeze, imagining she is Elaine the lovable, floating on a river down to Camelot. Hard, being a lily maid now her belly is swelling.

She remembers her belly reluctantly, not wanting to touch it, unwilling to acknowledge that it exists. Elaine the lily maid had no belly, surely, she thinks, forgetting that Galahad must have been born somehow. (Perhaps he rose out of the lake?) She imagines her belly as a sort of cavern, where something is growing in the darkness, something that is not hers, alien and unwelcome.

Only twelve months ago (fourteen, actually, but she is bad at numbers), she was Princess Elizabeth of Hibernia, dressed in pink satin, gossiping about the riding master with her friends, dancing with her brothers through the ruined arches of Westminster Cathedral, and eating too much cake at her seventeenth birthday party. Now, and she does not want to think about this so it remains at the edges of her mind, where unpleasant things, frogs and slugs, reside, she is a cavern with something growing inside her, something repugnant, something that is not hers, not the lily maid of Astolat's.

She reaches for a rose, an overblown Gloire de Dijon that, in a fit of temper, pierces her finger with its thorns. She cries out, sucks the blood from her finger, and flops down on the bank like a miserable child. The hem of her diaphanous dress begins to absorb the mud at the edge of the water.

III. The Magician

Wolfgang Magus places the rose he picked that morning in his buttonhole and looks at his reflection in the glass. He frowns, as his master Herr Doktor Ambrosius would have frowned, at the scarecrow in faded wool with a drooping gray mustache. A sad figure for a court magician.

"*Gott in Himmel,*" he says to himself, a childhood habit he has kept from nostalgia, for Wolfgang Magus is a reluctant atheist. He knows it is not God's fault but the King's, who pays him so little. If the King were to pay him, say, another shilling per week—but no, that too he would send to his sister, dying of consumption at a spa in Berne. His mind turns, painfully, from the memory of her face, white and drained, which already haunts him like a ghost.

He picks up a volume of Goethe's poems that he has carefully tied with a bit of pink ribbon and sighs. What sort of present is this, for the Princess's christening?

He enters the chapel with shy, stooping movements. It is full, and noisy with court gossip. As he proceeds up the aisle, he is swept by a duchess's train of peau de soie, poked by a viscountess's aigrette. The sword of a marquis smelling of Napoleon-water tangles in his legs, and he almost falls on a baroness, who stares at him through her lorgnette. He sidles through the crush until he comes to a corner of the chapel wall, where he takes refuge.

The christening has begun, he supposes, for he can hear the Archbishop droning in bad Latin, although he can see nothing from his corner but taxidermed birds and heads slick with macassar oil. Ah, if the Archbishop could have learned from Herr Doktor Ambrosius! His mind wanders, as it often does, to a house in Berlin and a laboratory smelling of strong soap, filled with braziers and alembics, books whose covers have been half-eaten by moths, a stuffed basilisk. He remembers his bed in the attic, and his sister, who worked as the Herr Doktor's housemaid so he could learn to be a magician. He sees her face on her pillow at the spa in Berne and thinks of her expensive medications.

What has he missed? The crowd is moving forward, and presents are being given: a rocking horse with a red leather saddle, a silver tumbler, a cap embroidered by the nuns of Iona. He hides the volume of Goethe behind his back.

Suddenly, he sees a face he recognizes. One day she came and sat beside him in the garden, and asked him about his sister. Her brother had died, he remembers, not long before, and as he described his loneliness, her eyes glazed over with tears. Even he, who understands little about court politics, knew she was the King's mistress.

She disappears behind the scented Marquis, then appears again, close to the altar where the Queen, awkwardly holding a linen bundle, is receiving the Princess's presents. The King has seen her, and frowns through his golden beard. Wolfgang Magus, who knows nothing about the feelings of a king toward his former mistress, wonders why he is angry.

She lifts her hand in a gesture that reminds him of the Archbishop. What fragrance is this, so sweet, so dark, that makes the brain clear, that makes the nostrils water? He instinctively tabulates: orris-root, oak gall, rose petal, dung of bat with a hint of vinegar.

Conversations hush, until even the baronets, clustered in a rustic clump at the back of the chapel, are silent.

She speaks: "This is the gift I give the Princess. On her seventeenth birthday she will prick her finger on the spindle of a spinning wheel and die."

Needless to describe the confusion that follows. Wolfgang Magus watches from its edge, chewing his mustache, worried, unhappy. How her eyes glazed, that day in the garden. Someone treads on his toes.

Then, unexpectedly, he is summoned. "Where is that blasted magician!" Gloved hands push him forward. He stands before the King, whose face has turned unattractively red. The Queen has fainted and a bottle of salts is waved under her nose. The Archbishop is holding the Princess, like a sack of barley he has accidentally caught.

"Is this magic, Magus, or just some bloody trick?"

Wolfgang Magus rubs his hands together. He has not stuttered since he was a child, but he answers, "Y-yes, Your Majesty. Magic." Sweet, dark, utterly magic. He can smell its power.

"Then get rid of it. Un-magic it. Do whatever you bloody well have to. Make it not be!"

Wolfgang Magus already knows that he will not be able to do so, but he says, without realizing that he is chewing his mustache in front of the King, "O-of course, Your Majesty."

IV. The King

What would you do, if you were James IV of Britannia, pacing across your council chamber floor before your councilors: the Count of Edinburgh, whose estates are larger than yours and include hillsides of uncut wood for which the French Emperor, who needs to refurbish his navy after the disastrous Indian campaign, would pay handsomely; the Earl of York, who can trace descent, albeit in the female line, from the Tudors; and the Archbishop, who has preached against marital infidelity in his cathedral at Aberdeen? The banner over your head, embroidered with the twelve-petaled rose of Britannia, reminds you that your claim to the throne rests tenuously on a former James's dalliance. Edinburgh's thinning hair, York's hanging jowl, the seams, edged with gold thread, where the Archbishop's robe has been let out, warn you, young as you are, with a beard that shines like a tangle of golden wires in the afternoon light, of your gouty future.

Britannia's economy depends on the wool trade, and spun wool sells for twice as much as unspun. Your income depends on the wool tax. The Queen, whom you seldom think of as Elizabeth, is young. You calculate: three months before she recovers from the birth, nine months before she can deliver another child. You might have an heir by next autumn.

"Well?" Edinburgh leans back in his chair, and you wish you could strangle his wrinkled neck.

You say, "I see no reason to destroy a thousand spinning wheels for one madwoman." Madeleine, her face puffed with sleep, her neck covered with a line of red spots where she lay on the pearl necklace you gave her the night before, one black hair tickling your ear. Clever of her, to choose a spinning wheel. "I rely entirely on Wolfgang Magus," whom you believe is a fraud. "Gentlemen, your fairy tales will have taught you that magic must be met with magic. One cannot fight a spell by altering material conditions."

Guffaws from the Archbishop, who is amused to think that he once read fairy tales.

You are a selfish man, James IV, and this is essentially your fault, but you have spoken the truth. Which, I suppose, is why you are the King.

V. The Queen Dowager

What is the girl doing? Playing at tug-of-war, evidently, and far too close to the stream. She'll tear her dress on the rosebushes. Careless, these young people, thinks the Queen Dowager. And who is she playing with? Young Lord Harry, who will one day be Count of Edinburgh. The Queen Dowager is proud of her keen eyesight and will not wear spectacles, although she is almost sixty-three.

What a pity the girl is so plain. The Queen Dowager jabs her needle into a black velvet slipper. Eyes like boiled gooseberries that always seem to be staring at you, and no discipline. Now in her day, thinks the Queen Dowager, remembering backboards and nuns who rapped your fingers with canes, in her day girls had discipline. Just look at the Queen: no discipline. Two miscarriages in ten years, and dead before her thirtieth birthday. Of course linen is so much cheaper now that the kingdoms are united. But if only her Jims (which is how she thinks of the King) could have married that nice German princess.

She jabs the needle again, pulls it out, jabs, knots. She holds up the slipper and then its pair, comparing the roses embroidered on each toe in stitches so even they seem to have been made by a machine. Quite perfect for her Jims, to keep his feet warm on the drafty palace floors.

A tearing sound, and a splash. The girl, of course, as the Queen Dowager could have warned you. Just look at her, with her skirt ripped up one side and her petticoat muddy to the knees.

"I do apologize, Madam. I assure you it's entirely my fault," says Lord Harry, bowing with the superfluous grace of a dancing master.

"It *is* all your fault," says the girl, trying to kick him.

"Alice!" says the Queen Dowager. Imagine the Queen wanting to name the girl Elaine. What a name, for a Princess of Britannia.

"But he took my book of poems and said he was going to throw it into the stream!"

"I'm perfectly sure he did no such thing. Go to your room at once. This is the sort of behavior I would expect from a chimney sweep."

"Then tell him to give my book back!"

Lord Harry bows again and holds out the battered volume. "It was always yours for the asking, Your Highness."

Alice turns away, and you see what the Queen Dowager cannot, despite her keen vision: Alice's eyes, slightly prominent, with irises that are indeed the color of gooseberries, have turned red at the corners, and her nose has begun to drip.

* * *

VI. The Spinning Wheel

It has never wanted to be an assassin. It remembers the cottage on the Isles where it was first made: the warmth of the hearth and the feel of its maker's hands, worn smooth from rubbing and lanolin.

It remembers the first words it heard: "And why are you carving roses on it, then?"

"This one's for a lady. Look how slender it is. It won't take your upland ram's wool. Yearling it'll have to be, for this one."

At night it heard the waves crashing on the rocks, and it listened as their sound mingled with the snoring of its maker and his wife. By day it heard the crying of the sea birds. But it remembered, as in a dream, the songs of inland birds and sunlight on a stone wall. Then the fishermen would come, and one would say, "What's that you're making there, Enoch? Is it for a midget, then?"

Its maker would stroke it with the tips of his fingers and answer, "Silent, lads. This one's for a lady. It'll spin yarn so fine that a shawl of it will slip through a wedding ring."

It has never wanted to be an assassin, and as it sits in a cottage to the south, listening as Madeleine mutters to herself, it remembers the sounds of seabirds and tries to forget that it was made, not to spin yarn so fine that a shawl of it will slip through a wedding ring, but to kill the King's daughter.

VII. The Princess

Alice climbs the tower stairs. She could avoid this perhaps, disguise herself as a peasant woman and beg her way to the Highlands, like a heroine in Scott's novels. But she does not want to avoid this, so she is climbing up the tower stairs on the morning of her seventeenth birthday, still in her nightgown and clutching a battered copy of Goethe's poems whose binding is so torn that the book is tied with pink ribbon to keep the pages together. Her feet are bare, because opening the shoe closet might have woken the Baroness, who has slept in her room since she was a child. Barefoot, she has walked silently past the sleeping guards, who are supposed to guard her today with particular care. She has walked past the Queen Dowager's drawing room thinking: if anyone hears me, I will be in disgrace.

She has spent a larger portion of her life in disgrace than out of it, and she remembers that she once thought of it as an imaginary country, Disgrace, with its own rivers and towns and trade routes. Would it be different if her mother were alive? She remembers a face creased from the folds of the pillow, and pale lips whispering to her about the lily maid of Astolat. It would, she supposes, have made no difference. She trips on a step and almost drops the book.

She has no reason to suppose, of course, that the Witch will be there, so early in the morning. But somehow, Alice hopes she will be.

She is, sitting on a low stool with a spinning wheel in front of her.

"Were you waiting for me?" asks Alice. It sounds silly—who else would the Witch be waiting for? But she can think of nothing else to say.

"I was." The Witch's voice is low and cadenced, and although she has wrinkles at the corners of her mouth and her hair has turned gray, she is still rather beautiful. She is not, exactly, what Alice expected.

"How did you know I was coming so early?"

The Witch smiles. "I've gotten rather good at magic. I sell fortunes for my living, you see. It's not much, just enough to buy bread and butter, and to rent a small cottage. But it amuses me, knowing things about people—their lives and their future."

"Do you know anything—about me?" Alice looks down at the book. What idiotic questions to be asking. Surely a heroine from Scott's novels would think of better.

The Witch nods, and sunlight catches the silver cross suspended from a chain around her neck. She says, "I'm sorry."

Alice understands, and her face flushes. "You mean that you've been watching all along. That you've known what it's been like, being the cursed princess." She turns and walks to the tower window, so the Witch will not see how her hands are shaking. "You know the other girls wouldn't play with me or touch my toys, that the boys would spit over their shoulders, to break the curse they said. Even the chambermaids would make the sign of the cross when I wasn't looking." She can feel tears where they always begin, at the corners of her eyes, and she leans out the window to cool her face. Far below, a gardener is crossing the courtyard, carrying a pair of pruning shears. She says, "Why didn't you remove the curse, then?"

"Magic doesn't work that way." The Witch's voice is sad. Alice turns around and sees that her cheeks are wet with tears. Alice steps toward her, trips again, and drops the book, which falls under the spinning wheel. The Witch picks it up and smiles as she examines the cover. "Of course, your Goethe. I always wondered what happened to Wolfgang Magus."

Alice thinks with relief: I'm not going to cry after all. "He went away, after his sister died. She had consumption, you know, for years and years. He was always sending her money for medicine. He wrote to me once after he left, from Berlin, to say that he had bought his old master's house. But I never heard from him again."

The Witch wipes her cheeks with the back of one hand. "I didn't know about his sister. I spoke to him once. He was a kind man."

Alice takes the book from her, then says, carefully, as though each word has to be placed in the correct order, "Do you think his spell will work? I mean, do you think I'll really sleep for a hundred years, rather than—you know?"

The Witch looks up, her cheeks still damp, but her face composed. "I can't answer that for you. You may simply be—preserved. In a pocket of time, as it were."

Alice tugs at the ribbon that binds the book together. "It doesn't matter, really. I don't think I care either way." She strokes the spinning wheel, which turns as she touches it. "How beautiful, as though it had been made just for me."

The Witch raises a hand, to stop her perhaps, or arrest time itself, but Alice places her finger on the spindle and presses until a drop of blood blossoms, as dark as the petal of a Cardinal de Richelieu, and runs into her palm.

Before she falls, she sees the Witch with her head bowed and her shoulders shaking. She thinks, for no reason she can remember, Elaine the fair, Elaine the lovable . . .

VIII. The Gardener

Long after, when the gardener has grown into an old man, he will tell his grandchildren about that day: skittish horses being harnessed by panicked grooms, nobles struggling with boxes while their valets carry armchairs and even bedsteads through the palace halls, the King in a pair of black velvet slippers shouting directions. The cooks leave the kettles whistling in the kitchen, the Queen Dowager leaves her jewels lying where she has dropped them while tripping over the hem of her nightgown. Everyone runs to escape the spreading lethargy that has already caught a canary in his cage, who makes soft noises as he settles into his feathers. The flowers are closing in the garden, and even the lobsters that the chef was planning to serve with melted butter for lunch have lain down in a corner of their tank.

In a few hours, the palace is left to the canary, and the lobsters, and the Princess lying on the floor of the tower.

He will say, "I was pruning a rosebush at the bottom of the tower that day. Look what I took away with me!" Then he will display a rose of the variety called Britannia, with its twelve petals half-open, still fresh and moist with dew. His granddaughter will say, "Oh, grandpa, you picked that in the garden just this morning!" His grandson, who is practical and wants to be an engineer, will say, "Grandpa, people can't sleep for a hundred years."

IX. The Tower

Let us get a historical perspective. When the tower was quite young, only a hovel really, a child knocked a stone out of its wall, and it gained an eye. With that eye it watched as the child's father, a chieftain, led his tribe against soldiers with metal breastplates and plumed helmets. Two lines met on the plain below: one regular, gleaming in the morning sun like the edge of a sword, the other ragged and blue like the crest of a wave. The wave washed over the sword, which splintered into a hundred pieces.

Time passed, and the tower gained a second story with a vertical eye as narrow as a staff. It watched a wooden structure grow beside it, in which men and cattle mingled indiscriminately. One morning it felt a prick, the point of an arrow. A bright flame blossomed from the beams of the wooden structure, men scattered, cattle screamed. One of its walls was singed, and it felt the wound as a distant heat. A castle rose, commanded by a man with eyebrows so blond that they were almost white, who caused the name Aelfric to be carved on the lintel of the tower. The castle's stone walls, pummelled with catapults, battered by rams, fell into fragments. From the hilltop a man watched, whose nose had been broken in childhood and remained perpetually crooked. When a palace rose from the broken rock, he caused the name D'Arblay to be carved on the lintel of the tower, beside a boar rampant.

Time passed, and a woman on a white horse rode through the village that had grown around the palace walls, followed by a retinue that stretched behind her like a scarf. At the palace gates, a Darbley grown rich on tobacco plantations in the New World presented her with the palace, in honor of her marriage to the Earl of Essex. The lintel of the tower was carved with the name Elizabeth I, and it gained a third story with a lead-paned window, through which it saw in facets like a fly. One morning it watched the Queen's son, who had been playing ball in the courtyard, fall to the ground with blood dripping from his nostrils. The windows of the palace were draped in black velvet, the Queen and her consort rode away with their retinue, and the village was deserted.

Time passed. Leaves turned red or gold, snow fell and melted into rivulets, young hawks took their first flight from the battlements. A rosebush grew at the foot of the tower: a hybrid, half wild rose, half Cuisse de Nymphe, with twelve petals and briary canes. One morning men rode up to the tower on horses whose hides were mottled with sweat. In its first story, where the chieftain's son had played, they talked of James III. Troops were coming from France, and the password was Britannia. As they left the tower, one of them plucked a flower from the rosebush. "Let this be our symbol," he said in the self-conscious voice of a man who thinks that his words will be recorded in history books. The tower thought it would be alone again, but by the time the leaves had turned, a procession rode up to the palace gates, waving banners embroidered with a twelve-petaled rose. Furniture arrived from France, fruit trees were planted, and the village streets were paved so that the hooves of cattle clopped on the stones.

It has stood a long time, that tower, watching the life around it shift and alter, like eddies in a stream. It looks down once again on a deserted village—but no, not entirely deserted. A woman still lives in a cottage at its edge. Her hair has turned white, but she works every day in her garden, gathering tomatoes and cutting back the mint. When the day is particularly warm, she brings out a spinning wheel and sits in the garden, spinning yarn so fine that a shawl of it will slip through a wedding ring. If the breezes come from the west, the tower can hear her humming, just above the humming that the wheel makes as it spins. Time passes, and she sits out in the garden less often, until one day it realizes that it has not seen her for many days, or perhaps years.

Sometimes at night it thinks it can hear the Princess breathing in her sleep.

X. The Hound

In a hundred years, only one creature comes to the palace: a hound whose coat is matted with dust. Along his back the hair has come out in tufts, exposing a mass of sores. He lopes unevenly: on one of his forepaws, the inner toes have been crushed.

He has run from a city reduced to stone skeletons and drifting piles of ash, dodging tanks, mortar fire, the rifles of farmers desperate for food. For weeks now, he has been loping along the dusty roads. When rain comes, he has curled himself under a tree. Afterward, he has drunk from puddles, then loped along again with mud drying in the hollows of his paws. Sometimes he has left the road and tried to catch rabbits in the fields, but his damaged paw prevents him from running quickly enough. He has smelled them in their burrows beneath the summer grasses, beneath the poppies and cornflowers, tantalizing, inaccessible.

This morning he has smelled something different, pungent, like spoiled meat: the smell of enchantment. He has left the road and entered the forest, finding his way through a tangle of briars. He has come to the village, loped up its cobbled streets and through the gates of the palace. His claws click on its stone floor.

What does he smell? A fragrance, drifting, indistinct, remembered from when he was a pup: bacon. There, through that doorway. He lopes into the Great Hall, where breakfast waits in chafing dishes. The eggs are still firm, their yolks plump and yellow, their whites delicately fried. Sausages sit in their own grease. The toast is crisp.

He leaves a streak of egg yolk and sausage grease on the table-cloth, which has remained pristine for half a century, and falls asleep in the Queen Dowager's drawing room, in a square of sunlight that has not faded the baroque carpet.

He lives happily ever after. Someone has to. As summer passes, he wanders through the palace gardens, digging in the flower beds and trying to catch the sleeping fish that float in the ornamental pools. One day he urinates on the side of the tower, from which the dark smell emanates, to show his disapproval. When he is hungry he eats from the side of beef hanging in the larder, the sausages and eggs remaining on the breakfast table, or the mice sleeping beneath the harpsichord. In autumn, he chases the leaves falling red and yellow over the lawns and manages to pull a lobster from the kitchen tank, although his teeth can barely crack its hard shell. He never figures out how to extract the canary from its cage. When winter comes, the stone floor sends an ache through his damaged paw, and he sleeps in the King's bed, under velvet covers.

When summer comes again, he is too old to run about the garden. He lies in the Queen Dowager's drawing room and dreams of being a pup, of warm hands and a voice that whispered "What a beautiful dog," and that magical thing called a ball. He dies, his stomach still full with the last of the poached eggs. A proper fairy tale should, perhaps, end here.

XI. The Prince

Here comes the Prince on a bulldozer. What did you expect? Things change in a hundred years.

Harry pulls back the break and wipes his forehead, which is glistening with sweat. He runs his fingers through blond hair that stands up like a shock of corn. It is just past noon, and the skin on his nose is already red and peeling.

Two acres, and he'll knock off for some beer and that liver and onion sandwich Madge made him this morning, whose grease, together with the juice of a large gherkin, is soaking its way through a brown paper wrapper and will soon stain the leather of his satchel. He leans back, looks at the tangle of briars that form the undergrowth in this part of the forest, and chews on the knuckle of his thumb.

Two acres in the middle of the forest, enough for some barley and a still. Hell of a good idea, he thinks, already imagining the bottles on their way to Amsterdam, already imagining his pals Mike and Steve

watching football on a color telly. Linoleum on the kitchen floor, like
Madge always wanted, and cigarettes from America. "Not that damn
rationed stuff," he says out loud, then looks around startled. What
kind of fool idiot talks to himself? He chews on the knuckle of his
thumb again. Twenty pounds to make the Police Commissioner look
the other way. Damn lucky Madge could lend them the money. The
bulldozer starts up again with a roar and the smell of diesel.

You don't like where this is going. What sort of prince is this,
with his liver and onion sandwich, his gherkin and beer? Forgive
me. I give you the only prince I can find, a direct descendant of the
Count of Edinburgh, himself descended from the Tudors, albeit in
the female line. Of course, all such titles have been abolished. This
is, after all, the Socialist Union of Britannia. If Harry knows he is a
prince, he certainly isn't telling Mike or Steve, who might sell him
out for a pack of American cigarettes. Even Madge can't be trust-
ed, though they've been sharing a flat in the commune's apartment
building for three years. Hell, she made a big enough fuss about the
distillery business.

The bulldozer's roar grows louder, then turns into a whine. The
front wheel is stuck in a ditch. Harry climbs down and looks at the
wheel. Damn, he'll have to get Mike and Steve. He kicks the wheel,
kicks a tree trunk and almost gets his foot caught in a briar, kicks the
wheel again.

Something flashes in the forest. Now what the hell is that? (You
and I know it is sunlight flashing from the faceted upper window
of the tower.) Harry opens his beer and swallows a mouthful of its
warm bitterness. Some damn poacher, walking around on his land.
(You and I remember that it belongs to the Socialist Union of Britannia.) He takes a bite of his liver and onion sandwich. Madge
shouldn't frown so much, he thinks, remembering her in her house-
coat, standing by the kitchen sink. She's getting wrinkles on her forehead. Should he fetch Mike and Steve? But the beer in his stomach,
warm, bitter, tells him that he doesn't need Mike and Steve, because
he can damn well handle any damn poacher himself. He bites into
the gherkin.

Stay away, Prince Harry. Stay away from the forest full of briars.
The Princess is not for you. You will never stumble up the tower
stairs, smelling of beer; never leave a smear of mingled grease and
sweat on her mouth; never take her away (thinking, Madge's rump is

getting too damn broad) to fry your liver and onions and empty your ashtray of cigarette butts and iron your briefs.

At least, I hope not.

XII. The Rose

Let us go back to the beginning: petals fall. Unpruned for a hundred years, the rosebush has climbed to the top of the tower. A cane of it has found a chink in the tower window, and it has grown into the room where the Princess lies. It has formed a canopy over her, a network of canes now covered with blossoms, and their petals fall slowly in the still air. Her nightgown is covered with petals: this summer's, pink and fragrant, and those of summers past, like bits of torn parchment curling at the edges.

While everything in the palace has been suspended in a pool of time without ripples or eddies, it has responded to the seasons. Its roots go down to dark caverns which are the homes of moles and worms, and curl around a bronze helmet that is now little more than rust. More than two hundred years ago, it was rather carelessly chosen as the emblem of a nation. Almost a hundred years ago, Madeleine plucked a petal of it for her magic spell. Wolfgang Magus picked a blossom of it for his buttonhole, which fell in the chapel and was trampled under a succession of court heels and cavalry boots. A spindle was carved from its dead and hardened wood. Half a century ago, a dusty hound urinated on its roots. From its seeds, dispersed by birds who have eaten its orange hips, has grown the tangle of briars that surround the palace, which have already torn the Prince's work pants and left a gash on his right shoulder. If you listen, you can hear him cursing.

It can tell us how the story ends. Does the Prince emerge from the forest, his shirtsleeve stained with blood? The briars of the forest know. Does the Witch lie dead, or does she still sit by the small-paned window of her cottage, contemplating a solitary pearl that glows in the wrinkled palm of her hand like a miniature moon? The spinning wheel knows, and surely its wood will speak to the wood from which it was made. Is the Princess breathing? Perhaps she has been sleeping for a hundred years, and the petals that have settled under her nostrils flutter each time she exhales. Perhaps she has not been sleeping, perhaps she is an exquisitely preserved corpse, and the petals under her nostrils never quiver. The rose can tell us, but it will not. The wind sets its leaves stirring, and petals fall, and it whispers to us: you must find your own ending.

This is mine. The Prince trips over an oak log, falls into a fairy ring, and disappears. (He is forced to wash miniature clothes, and pinched when he complains.) Alice stretches and brushes the rose petals from her nightgown. She makes her way to the Great Hall and eats what is left in the breakfast dishes: porridge with brown sugar. She walks through the streets of the village, wondering at the silence, then hears a humming. Following it, she comes to a cottage at the village edge where Madeleine, her hair now completely white, sits and spins in her garden. Witches, you know, are extraordinarily long-lived. Alice says, "Good morning," and Madeleine asks, "Would you like some breakfast?" Alice says, "I've had some, thank you." Then the Witch spins while the Princess reads Goethe, and the spinning wheel produces yarn so fine that a shawl of it will slip through a wedding ring.

Will it come to pass? I do not know. I am waiting, like you, for the canary to lift its head from under its wing, for the Empress Josephine to open in the garden, for a sounds that will tell us someone, somewhere, is awake.

Thorns and Briars

I locked my heart in a box
and put that box on a shelf
high in the room of a house
surrounded by thorns and briars.

They parted to let me through,
then closed behind me again,
and I went out into the world
unafraid, because heartless.

I did the work I was told,
completed the tasks I was given,
nodded and smiled, so they thought
I was such a reliable girl.

But all that time, my heart
was beating in a box
made of some fancy wood
inlaid with mother-of-pearl.

I gathered credentials, gained
titles and honors, was granted
suitable recompense—
while the thorns and briars grew higher

until you could no longer see
the small gray house behind,
and my heart was safe on the shelf
from either theft or scrutiny.

The thorns and briars will only
part for the one predestined
to rescue my heart from the box—
so someday, I'll return

and open the gate. Then the tangle
of thorns and briars will part
to make a path to the door
of the house, and all the roses,

the simple dog-roses, the elegant
albas, gallicas, portlands
on those canes will burst into bloom,
white and pink and red.

In the room, surrounded by books
and dust, I will take the box
off the shelf and reclaim my heart
as preordained.

Rose Child

Wandering among the roses in my garden,
I found a child, only five inches tall,
under a Madam Hardy. She was standing
on mulch, leaning against one of the rose canes.
I bent down to look at her, and she looked back
fearlessly. She was lean and brown, dressed
in a dormouse skin, cleverly sewn together.
She raised one hand, and I saw that she was armed
with a long, sharp thorn. She was not threatening me,
just showing me that she was not defenseless.
She shook the cane, and rose petals fell down
around her like summer snow. What should I do?
She was a child, but clearly self-sufficient,
in no need of help from me. So I did nothing.

Every morning, when I went to check the roses
for blackspot or Japanese beetles, I would see her
or traces of her—aphids speared on a thorn,
a pile of raspberries pilfered from my garden.
I didn't mind—she could take what she wanted.
Would it be wrong of me to leave her something?
And what would be useful to her? String, I thought.
Toothpicks, pieces of felt, a cut-up apple.
I would leave them under the blossoming Cuisse de Nymphe
or Cardinal Richelieu. They were always taken.
One morning I found a Japanese beetle spitted
on a toothpick, and the next morning I found two.
I think it was her way of thanking me.

She must have noticed what they do to roses,
how they eat the leaves and petals, chewing through them
until they are only a series of ragged holes
held together by a spiderweb of veins.

I did not see her again for a long time,
just tiny footsteps where I had raked the soil.
But one day I found her lying under the birdbath.
Immediately, I could tell there was something wrong;
she was pale, her breathing irregular, in quick gasps.
She lay with her arms wrapped around her torso, the way
you do when you're trying to hold yourself together.
What should I have done? We are always told not to touch
the wild things: abandoned fawns aren't really abandoned,
mother birds may return for fallen fledglings.
But she was a girl—a wild girl, but still human.

I put her in a shoebox lined with batting
and carried her up to the porch, which had a screen
to keep out insects, but was not indoors, exactly.
I brought her the sorts of things I thought she ate
in the wilderness of my garden: raspberries,
sliced peaches, lettuce, peas, asparagus sprouts,
even a frog I had to spear myself,
but I had seen her thorn, so I knew she hunted.
She ate it raw, all except the skin and bones.
Nothing seemed to help. Each day she would eat
less, sleep more. Slowly, she grew sicker,
coughing and feverish, with the typical symptoms
of a respiratory infection, something viral
that even her strong system couldn't fight off.
One day, she stopped eating altogether.
She drank water from a thimble, that was all.

Next morning, I sat with her as she closed her eyes,
and then it was over, as quickly and peacefully
as a bird flies from its nest. I buried her
by the edge of the woods, under a stand of maples.

I put a stone there, gray with a vein of quartz.
Then winter came, and I was sick myself;
at my age, I don't get over these things as easily
as I used to. Meanwhile, the garden lay dormant, snowbound.
I mostly stared at it from the kitchen window.

When spring came again, and all the snow was melted,
I walked around to survey what had been damaged.
The rose canes were dry and brown. I'd have to prune them
so new green shoots could spring from above the graft
to form flowering mid-summer arches. The vegetable garden
was covered with burlap. I peeled it back to see
what had survived underneath: mostly beets and turnips.
Almost as an afterthought, I walked to her grave.
In front of the stone was heaped a strange assortment:
acorns, a piece of faded ribbon, the cap
from a soda bottle, several sharpened sticks,
a bright blue plastic button. I started to sweep
it away as rubbish, then suddenly realized
that no, these were grave goods. As ancient tribes would honor
their dead by burying them with weapons, supplies
for the afterlife. Later that day, I brought
the thimble she had drunk from and left it there,
like a chalice on a church alter. Every morning
I'd go and leave something: berries, and when the roses
had started blooming again, the finest blossom
I could find that morning, fragrant, still covered with dew.

It was mid-summer before I started to see them,
the wild children, no larger than she had been,
dressed in skins, with weapons just like hers.
Now, when I'm in the garden deadheading the lilies
or cutting back the mint, sometimes I'll see one,
sitting on the old stone wall, enjoying the sunshine,
never speaking, just being companionable.
Or one will be leaning on a tomato trellis,
arms crossed, watching the birds in the lilac bushes.
Sometimes I'll leave out something they might find useful,

a ragged handkerchief, a knitting needle
that would make a fine spear. But I try not to interfere
in their lives—some things should be left as they are;
at my age I've learned that. I hope eventually,
when I'm buried by the edge of the woods myself,
which is what I've arranged for, they will come and visit,
leaving bits of ribbon, or buttons, or maybe a rose
every once in a while. It makes the thought of death
easier, somehow, that they would still be climbing
up the branches of the apple tree, or fishing
in the pond, or maybe dancing under the moon
if indeed they do that—I've never seen them,
just tiny tracks in the newly prepared bed
where I was planning to sow the radish seeds.

If they could visit me, just once or twice,
even if there's nothing of me left
to know or care—I'd like that.

Thumbelina

Sometimes I would like to be very small
so I could curl into a snail's shell
or a seashell: abalone, nautilus,
even an oyster shell. I would let the oyster
cover me with layer on layer of nacre,
come out shining.

Sometimes I would like to be very small
so I could hide myself inside a flower,
between the petals of a tulip or crocus,
inside purple or crimson walls, like a genie
in her bottle. I would emerge covered
with pollen, riding a bee.

Sometimes I would like to be small enough
to live in the hollow of a tree, like a bird
or squirrel. I would dress in leaves, eat acorns,
make a coat of felted fur. I would live alone,
hiding, hiding, always hiding,
because the world is full of large things
that are too large, too loud.
Over them, I can't hear the sea
whispering, the beat of a sparrow's wings,
the annoyed chuff of a robin.

I would like to be small enough
to hear the dawn breaking, the tulip opening,
the sand as it shifts under each tide,
the long dream of rocks.

Blanchefleur

They called him Idiot.

He was the miller's son, and he had never been good for much. At least not since his mother's death, when he was twelve years old. He had found her floating, face-down, in the millpond, and his cries had brought his father's men. When they had turned her over, he had seen her face, pale and bloated, before someone had said, "Not in front of the child!" and they had hurried him away. He had never seen her again, just the wooden coffin going into the ground, and after that, the gray stone in the churchyard where, every Sunday, he and his father left whatever was in season—a bunch of violets, sprays of the wild roses that grew by the forest edge, tall lilies from beside the mill stream. In winter, they left holly branches red with berries.

Before her death, he had been a laughing, affectionate child. After her death, he became solitary. He would no longer play with his friends from school, and eventually they began to ignore him. He would no longer speak even to his father, and anyway the miller was a quiet man who, after his wife's death, grew more silent. He was so broken, so bereft, by the loss of his wife that he could barely look at the son who had her golden hair, her eyes the color of spring leaves. Often they would go a whole day, saying no more than a few sentences to each other.

He went to school, but he never seemed to learn—he would stare out the window or, if called upon, shake his head and refuse to answer. Once, the teacher rapped his knuckles for it, but he simply looked at her with those eyes, which were so much like his mother's. The teacher turned away, ashamed of herself, and after that she left him alone, telling herself that at least he was sitting in the schoolroom rather than loafing about the fields.

He learned nothing, he did nothing. When his father told him to do the work of the mill, he did it so badly that the water flowing through the sluice gates was either too fast or slow, or the large mill-stones that grind the grain were too close together or far apart, or he took the wrong amount of grain in payment from the farmers who came to grind their wheat. Finally, the miller hired another man, and his son wandered about the countryside, sometimes sleeping under the stars, eating berries from the hedges when he could find them. He would come home dirty, with scratches on his arms and brambles in his hair. And his father, rather than scolding him, would look away.

If anyone had looked closely, they would have seen that he was clever at carving pieces of wood into whistles and seemed to know how to call all the birds. Also, he knew the paths through the countryside and could tell the time by the position of the sun and moon on each day of the year, his direction by the stars. He knew the track and spoor of every animal, what tree each leaf came from by its shape. He knew which mushrooms were poisonous and how to find water under the ground. But no one did look closely.

It was the other schoolboys, most of whom had once been his friends, who started calling him Idiot. At first it was Idiot Ivan, but soon it was simply Idiot, and it spread through the village until people forgot he had ever been called Ivan. Farmers would call to him, cheerfully enough, "Good morning, Idiot!" They meant no insult by it. In villages, people like knowing who you are. The boy was clearly an idiot, so let him be called that. And so he was.

No one noticed that under the dirt, and despite the rags he wore, he had grown into a large, handsome boy. He should have had sweethearts, but the village girls assumed he was slow and had no prospects, even though he was the miller's son. So he was always alone, and the truth was, he seemed to prefer it.

The miller was the only one who still called him Ivan, although he had given his son up as hopeless, and even he secretly believed that the boy was slow and stupid.

This was how things stood when the miller rode to market to buy a new horse. The market was held in the nearest town, on a fine summer day that was also the feast-day of Saint Ivan, so the town was filled with stalls selling livestock, vegetables from the local farms, leather and rope harnesses, embroidered linen, woven baskets. Men and women in smocks lined up to hire themselves for the coming harvest. There were strolling players with fiddles or pipes, dancers on a wooden platform, and a great deal of beer—which the miller drank from a tankard.

The market went well for him. He found a horse for less money than he thought he would have to spend, and while he was paying for his beer, one of the maids from the tavern winked at him. She was plump, with sunburnt cheeks, and she poured his beer neatly, leaving a head of foam that just reached the top of the tankard. He had not thought of women, not in that way, since his wife had drowned. She had been one of those magical women, beautiful as the dawn, as slight as a willow-bough and with a voice like birds singing, that are perhaps too delicate for this world. That kind of woman gets into a man's blood. But lately he had started to notice once again that other women existed, and there were other things in the world than running a mill. Like his son, who was a great worry to him. What would the idiot—Ivan, he reminded himself—what would he do when the his father was gone, as we must all go someday? Would he be able to take care of himself?

He had saddled his horse and was fastening a rope to his saddle so the new horse could be led, when he heard a voice he recognized from many years ago. "Hello, Stephen Miller," it said.

He turned around and bowed. "Hello, Lady."

She was tall and pale, with long gray hair that hung to the backs of her knees, although she did not look older than when he had last seen her, at his wedding. She wore a gray linen dress that, although it was midsummer, reminded him of winter.

"How is my nephew? This is his name day, is it not?"

"It is, Lady. As to how he is—" The miller told her. He might not have, if the beer had not loosened his tongue, for he was a proud man and he did not want his sister-in-law to think that his son was doing badly. But with the beer and his worries, it all came out—the days Ivan spent staring out of windows or walking through the country-side, how the local farmers thought of him, even that name—Idiot.

"I warned you that no good comes of a mortal marrying a fairy woman," said the Lady. "But those in love never listen. Send my nephew to me. I will make him my apprentice for three years, and at the end of that time we shall see. For his wages, you may take this."

She handed him a purse. He bowed in acknowledgment, saying, "I thank you for your generosity—" but when he straightened again, she was already walking away from him. Just before leaving the inn yard, she turned back for a moment and said, "The Castle in the Forest, remember. I will expect him in three days' time."

The miller nodded, although she had already turned away again. As he rode home, he looked into the purse she had given him—in it was a handful of leaves. He wondered how he was going to tell his son about the bargain he had made. But when he reached home, the boy was sitting at the kitchen table whittling something out of wood, and he simply said, "I have apprenticed you for three years to your aunt, the Lady of the Forest. She expects you in three days' time."

The boy did not say a word. But the next morning, he put all of his possessions—they were few enough—into a satchel, which he slung over his shoulder. And he set out.

In three days' time, Ivan walked through the forest, blowing on the whistle he had carved. He could hear birds calling to each other in the forest. He whistled to them, and they whistled back. He did not know how long his journey would take—if you set out for the Castle in the Forest, it can take you a day, or a week, or the rest of your life. But the Lady had said she expected him in three days, so he thought he would reach the Castle by the end of the day at the latest.

Before he left, his father had looked again in the purse that the Lady had given him. In it was a pile of gold coins—as the miller had expected, for that is the way fairy money works. "I will keep this for you," his father had said. "When you come back, you will be old enough to marry, and with such a fortune, any of the local girls will take you. I do not know what you will do as the Lady's apprentice, but I hope you will come back fit to run a mill."

Ivan had simply nodded, slung his satchel over his shoulder, and gone.

Just as he was wondering if he would indeed find the castle that day, for the sun was beginning to set, he saw it through the trees, its turrets rising above a high stone wall.

He went up to the wall and knocked at the wooden door that was the only way in. It opened, seemingly by itself. In the doorway stood a white cat.

"Are you the Idiot?" she asked.

"I suppose so," he said, speaking for the first time in three days.

"That's what I thought," she said. "You certainly look the part. Well, come in then, and follow me."

He followed her through the doorway and along a path that led through the castle gardens. He had never seen such gardens, although in school his teacher had once described the gardens that surrounded the King's castle, which she had visited on holiday. There were fountains set in green lawns, with stone fish spouting water. There were box hedges, and topiaries carved into the shapes of birds, rabbits, mice. There were pools filled with waterlilies, in which he could see real fish, silver and orange. There were arched trellises from which roses hung down in profusion, and an orchard with fruit trees. He could even see a kitchen garden, with vegetables in neat rows. And all through the gardens, he could see cats, pruning the hedges, tying back the roses, raking the earth in the flower beds.

It was the strangest sight he had ever seen, and for the first time it occurred to him that being the Lady's apprentice would be an adventure—the first of his life.

The path took them to the door of the castle, which swung open as they approached. An orange tabby walked out and stood waiting at the top of the steps.

"Hello, Marmalade," said the white cat.

"Good evening, Miss Blanchefleur," he replied. "Is this the young man Her Ladyship is expecting?"

"As far as I can tell," she said. "Although what my mother would want with such an unprepossessing specimen, I don't know."

Marmalade bowed to Ivan and said, "Welcome, Ivan Miller. Her Ladyship is waiting in the solar."

Ivan expected the white cat, whose name seemed to be Blanchefleur, to leave him with Marmalade, but instead she followed them through the doorway, then through a great hall whose walls were hung with tapestries showing cats sitting in gardens, climbing trees, hunting rabbits, catching fish. Here too there were cats, setting out bowls on two long wooden tables, and on a shorter table set on a dais at the end of the room. As Marmalade passed, they nodded, and a gray cat who seemed to be directing their activities said, "We're almost ready, Mr. Marmalade. The birds are nicely roasted, and the mint sauce is really a treat if I say so myself."

"Excellent, Mrs. Pebbles. I can't tell you how much I'm looking forward to those birds. Tailcatcher said he caught them himself."

"Well, with a little help!" said Mrs. Pebbles, acerbically. "He doesn't go on the hunt alone, does he now, Mr. Marmalade? Oh, begging your pardon, Miss," she said when she saw Blanchefleur. "I didn't know you were there."

"I couldn't care less what you say about him," said Blanchefleur, with a sniff and a twitch of her tail. "He's nothing to me."

"As you say, Miss," said Mrs. Pebbles, not sounding particularly convinced.

At the back of the great hall was another, smaller door that led to a long hallway. Ivan was startled when, at the end of the hallway, which had been rather dark, they emerged into a room filled with sunlight. It had several windows looking out onto a green lawn, and scattered around the room were low cushions, on which cats sat engaged in various tasks. Some were carding wool, some were spinning it on drop spindles, some were plying the yarn or winding it into skeins. In a chair by one of the windows sat the Lady, with a piece of embroidery in her lap. One of the cats was reading a book aloud, but stopped when they entered.

"My Lady, this is Ivan Miller, your new apprentice," said Marmalade.

"Otherwise known as the Idiot," said Blanchefleur. "And he seems to deserve the name. He's said nothing for himself all this time."

"My dear, you should be polite to your cousin," said the Lady. "Ivan, you've already met my daughter, Blanchefleur, and Marmalade, who takes such marvelous care of us all. These are my ladies-in-waiting: Elderberry, Twilight, Snowy, Whiskers, and Fluff. My daughter tells me you have nothing to say for yourself. Is that true?"

Ivan stared at her, sitting in her chair, surrounded by cats. She had green eyes, and although her gray hair hung down to the floor, she reminded him of his mother. "Yes, ma'am," he said.

She looked at him for a moment, appraisingly. Then she said, "Very well. I will send you where you need not say anything. Just this morning I received a letter from an old friend of mine, Professor Owl. He is compiling an Encyclopedia of All Knowledge, but he is old and feels arthritis terribly in his legs. He can no longer write the entries himself. For the first year of your apprenticeship, you will go to Professor Owl in the Eastern Waste and help him with his Encyclopedia. Do you think you can do that, nephew?"

"It's all the same to me," said Ivan. It was obvious that no one wanted him here, just as no one had wanted him at the mill. What did it matter where he went?

"Then you shall set out tomorrow morning," said the Lady. "Tonight you shall join us for dinner. Are the preparations ready, Marmalade?"

"Almost, My Lady," said the orange cat.

"How will I find this Professor Owl?" asked Ivan.

"Blanchefleur will take you," said the Lady.

"You can't be serious!" said Blanchefleur. "He's an idiot, and he stinks like a pigsty."

"Then show him the bathroom, where he can draw himself a bath," said the Lady. "And give him new clothes to wear. Those are too ragged even for Professor Owl, I think."

"Come on, you," said Blanchefleur, clearly disgusted. He followed her out of the room and up a flight of stairs, to a bathroom with a large tub on four clawed legs. He had never seen anything quite like it before. At the mill, he had often washed under the kitchen spigot. After she had left, he filled it with hot water that came out of a tap and slipped into it until the water was up to his chin.

What a strange day it had been. Three days ago he had left his father's house and the life he had always lived, a life that required almost nothing of him: no thought, no effort. And now here he was, in a castle filled with talking cats. And tomorrow he would start for another place, one that might be even stranger. When Blanchefleur had taunted him by telling the Lady that he had nothing to say for himself, he had wanted to say—what? Something that would have made her less disdainful. But what could he say for himself, after all?

With the piece of soap, he washed himself more carefully than he had ever before in his life. She had said that he smelled like a pigsty, and he had spent the night before last sleeping on a haystack that was, indeed, near a pen where several pigs had grunted in their dreams. Last night, he had slept in the forest, but he supposed the smell still lingered—particularly to a cat's nose. For the first time in years, he felt a sense of shame.

He dried himself and put on the clothes she had left for him. He went back down the stairs, toward the sound of music, and found his way to the great hall. It was lit with torches, and sitting at the two long tables were cats of all colors: black and brindled and tortoiseshell and piebald, with short hair and long. Sitting on the dais were the Lady, with Blanchefleur beside her, and a large yellow and brown cat who was striped like a tiger. He stood in the doorway, feeling self-conscious.

The Lady saw him across the room and motioned for him to come over. He walked to the dais and bowed before it, because that seemed the appropriate thing to do. She said, "That was courteous, nephew. Now come sit with us. Tailcatcher, you will not mind giving your seat to Ivan, will you?"

"Of course not, My Lady," said the striped cat in a tone that indicated he did indeed mind, very much.

Ivan took his place, and Marmalade brought him a dish of roast starlings, with a green sauce that smelled like catmint. It was good, although relatively flavorless. The cats, evidently, did not use salt in their cooking. Halfway through the meal, he was startled to realize that the cats were conversing with one another and nodding politely, as though they were a roomful of ordinary people. He was probably the only silent one in the entire room. Several times he noticed Blanchefleur giving him exasperated looks.

When he had finished eating, the Lady said, "I think it's time to dance." She clapped her hands, and suddenly Ivan heard music. He wondered where it was coming from, then noticed a group of cats at the far end of the room playing, more skillfully than he had supposed possible, a fife, a viol, a tabor, and other instruments he could not identify, one of which curved like a long snake. The cats that had been sitting at the long tables moved them to the sides of the room, then formed two lines in the center. He had seen a line dance before, at one of the village fairs, but he had never seen one danced as gracefully as it was by the cats. They wove in and out, each line breaking and reforming in intricate patterns.

"Aren't you going to ask your cousin to dance?" said the Lady, leaning over to him.

"What? Oh," he said, feeling foolish. How could he dance with a cat? But the Lady was looking at him, waiting. "Would you like to dance?" he asked Blanchefleur.

"Not particularly," she said, looking at him with disdain. "Oh, all right, Mother! You don't have to pull my tail."

He wiped his mouth and hands on a napkin, then followed Blanchefleur to the dance floor and joined at the end of the line, feeling large and clumsy, trying to follow the steps and not tread on any paws. It did not help that, just when he was beginning to feel as though he was learning the steps, he saw Tailcatcher glaring at him from across the room. He danced several times, once with

Blanchefleur, once with Mrs. Pebbles, who must have taken pity on him, and once with Fluff, who told him that it was a pleasure to dance with such a handsome young man and seemed to mean it. He managed to step on only one set of paws, belonging to a tabby tomcat who said, "Do that again, Sir, and I'll send you my second in the morning," but was mollified when Ivan apologized sincerely and at length. After that, he insisted on sitting down until the feast was over and he could go to bed.

The next morning, he woke and wondered if it was all a dream, but no—there he was, lying in a curtained bed in the Lady's castle. And there was Blanchefleur, sitting in a nearby chair, saying, "About time you woke up. We need to get started if we're going to make the Eastern Waste by nightfall."

Ivan got out of bed, vaguely embarrassed to be seen in his night-shirt, then reminded himself that she was just a cat. He put on the clothes he had been given last night, then found his satchel on a dresser. All of his old clothes were gone, replaced by new ones. In the satchel he also found a loaf of bread, a hunk of cheese, a flask of wine, and a shiny new knife with a horn handle.

"I should thank the Lady for all these things," he said.

"That's the first sensible thing you've said since you got here," said Blanchefleur. "But she's gone to see my father, and won't be back for three days. And we have to get going. So hurry up already!"

The Lady's castle was located in a forest called the Wolfwald. To the north, it stretched for miles, and parts of it were so thick that almost no sunlight reached the forest floor. At the foot of the northern mountains, wolves still roamed. But around the castle it was less dense. Ivan and Blanchefleur walked along a path strewn with oak leaves, through filtered sunlight. Ivan was silent, in part because he was accustomed to silence, in part because he did not know what to say to the white cat. Blanchefleur seemed much more interested in chasing insects, and even dead leaves, than in talking to him.

They stopped to rest when the sun was directly overhead. The forest had changed: the trees were shorter and spaced more widely apart, mostly pines rather than the oaks and beeches around the Lady's castle. Ahead of him, Ivan could see a different sort of landscape: bare, except for the occasional twisted trees and clumps of grass. It was dry, rocky, strewn with boulders.

"That's the Eastern Waste," said Blanchefleur.

"The ground will be too hard for your paws," said Ivan. "I can carry you."

"I'll do just fine, thank you," she said with a sniff. But after an hour of walking over the rocky ground, Ivan saw that she was limping. "Come on," he said. "If you hate the thought of me carrying you so much, pretend I'm a horse."

"A jackass is more like it," she said. But she let him pick her up and carry her, with her paws on his shoulder so she could look around. Occasionally, her whiskers tickled his ear.

The sun traveled across the sky, and hours passed, and still he walked though that rocky landscape, until his feet hurt. But he would not admit he was in pain, not with Blanchefleur perched on his shoulder. At last, after a region of low cliffs and defiles, they came to a broad plain that was nothing but stones. In the middle of the plain rose a stone tower.

"That's it," said Blanchefleur. "That's Professor Owl's home."

"Finally," said Ivan under his breath. He had been feeling as though he would fall over from sheer tiredness. He took a deep breath and started for the tower. But before he reached it, he asked the question he had been wanting to ask all day, but had not dared to. "Blanchefleur, who is your father?"

"The man who lives in the moon," she said. "Can you hurry up? I haven't had a meal since that mouse at lunch, and I'm getting hungry."

"He's an owl," said Ivan.

"Of course he's an owl," said Blanchefleur. "What did you think he would be?"

Professor Owl was in fact an owl, the largest Ivan has ever seen, with brown and white feathers. When they entered the tower, which was round and had one room on each level, with stairs curling around the outer wall, he said, "Welcome, welcome. Blanchefleur, I haven't seen you since you were a kitten. And this must be the assistant the Lady has so graciously sent me. Welcome, boy. I hope you know how to write a good, clear hand."

"His name is Idiot," said Blanchefleur.

"My name is Ivan," said Ivan.

"Yes, yes," said Professor Owl, paying no attention to them whatsoever. "Here, then, is my life's work. The Encyclopedia."

It was an enormous book, taller than Ivan himself, resting on a large stand at the far end of the room. In the middle of the room was a wooden table, and around the circular walls were file cabinets, all the way up to the ceiling.

"It's much too heavy to open by hand—or foot," said Professor Owl. "But if you tell the Encyclopedia what you're looking for, it will open to that entry."

"Mouse," said Blanchefleur. And sure enough, as she spoke, the pages of the Encyclopedia turned as though by magic (*although it probably is magic*, thought Ivan) to a page with an entry titled *Mouse*.

"Let's see, let's see," said Professor Owl, peering at the page. "'The bright and active, although mischievous, little animal known to us by the name of Mouse and its close relative the Rat are the most familiar and also the most typical members of the Murinae, a sub-family containing about two hundred and fifty species assignable to no less than eighteen distinct genera, all of which, however, are so superficially alike that the English names rat or mouse would be fairly appropriate to any of them.' Well, that seems accurate, doesn't it?"

"Does it say how they taste?" asked Blanchefleur.

"The Encyclopedia is connected to five others," said Professor Owl, turning to Ivan. "One is in the Library of Alexandria, one in the Hagia Sophia in Constantinople, one in the Sorbonne, one in the British Museum, and one in the New York Public Library. It is the only Encyclopedia of All Knowledge, and as you can imagine, it takes all my time to keep it up to date. I've devoted my life to it. But since I've developed arthritis in my legs (and Ivan could see that indeed, the owl's legs looked more knobby than they ought to), it's been difficult for me to write my updates. So I'm grateful to the Lady for sending you. Here is where you will work." He pointed to the table with his clawed foot. On it was a large pile of paper, each page filled with scribbled notes.

"These are the notes I've made indicating what should be updated and how. If you'll look at the page on top of the pile, for instance, you'll see that the entry on Justice needs to be updated. There have been, in the last month alone, five important examples of injustice, from the imprisonment of a priest who criticized the Generalissimo to a boy who was deprived of his supper when his mother wrongly accused him of stealing a mince pie. You must add each example to the entry under Justice—Injustice—Examples. The entry itself can be found in one of the cabinets along the wall—I believe it's the twenty-sixth row from the door, eight cabinets up. Of course I can't possibly include every example of injustice—there are hundreds every hour. I only include the ones that most clearly illustrated the concept. And here are my notes on a species of wild rose newly discovered in the mountains of Cathay. That will go under Rose—Wild—Species. Do you understand, boy? You are to look at my notes and add whatever information is necessary to update the entry, writing directly on the file. The Encyclopedia itself will incorporate your update, turning it into typescript, but you must make your letters clearly. And no spelling errors! Now, it's almost nightfall, and I understand that humans have defective vision, so I suggest you sleep until dawn, when you can get up and start working on these notes as well as the ones I'll be writing overnight."

"Professor," said Blanchefleur, "we haven't had dinner."

"Dinner?" said Professor Owl. "Of course, of course. I wouldn't want you to go hungry. There are some mice and birds in the cupboard. I caught them just last night. You're certainly welcome to them."

"Human beings can't eat mice and birds," said Blanchefleur. "They have to cook their food."

"Yes, yes, of course," said Professor Owl. "An inefficient system, I must say. I believe I had—but where did I put it?" He turned around, looking perplexed, then opened the door of a closet under the stairs. He poked his head in, and then tossed out several things, so both Ivan and Blanchefleur had to dodge them. A pith helmet, a butterfly net, and a pair of red flannel underwear for what must have been a very tall man. "Yes, here is it. But you'll have to help me with it."

"It" was a large iron kettle. Ivan helped the owl pull it out of the closet and place it on the long wooden table. He looked into it, not knowing what to expect, but it was empty.

"It's a magic kettle, of course," said Professor Owl. "I seem to remember that it makes soup. You can sleep on the second floor. The third is my study, and I hope you will refrain from disturbing me during daylight hours, when I will be very busy indeed. Now, if you don't mind, I'm going out for a bit of a hunt. I do hope you will be useful to me. My last apprentice was a disappointment." He waddled comically across the floor and up the stairs.

"These scholarly types aren't much for small talk," said Blanchefleur.

"I thought he was going out?" said Ivan.

"He is," said Blanchefleur. "You don't think he's just going to walk out the door, do you? He's an owl. He's going to launch himself from one of the tower windows."

Ivan looked into the kettle again. Still empty. "Do you really think it's magic?" he asked. He had eaten the bread and cheese a long time ago, and his stomach was starting to growl.

"Try some magic words," said Blanchefleur.

"Abracadabra," he said. "Open Sesame." What other magic words had he learned in school? If he remembered correctly, magic had not been a regular part of the curriculum.

"You really are an idiot," said Blanchefleur. She sprang onto the table, then sat next to the kettle. "Dear Kettle," she said. "We've been told of your magical powers in soup-making, and are eager to taste your culinary delights. Will you please make us some soup? Any flavor, your choice, but not onion because his breath is pungent enough already."

From the bottom, the kettle filled with something that bubbled and had a delicious aroma. "There you go," said Blanchefleur. "Magical items have feelings, you know. They need to be asked nicely. Abracadabra indeed!"

"I still need a spoon," said Ivan.

"With all you require for nourishment, I wonder that you're still alive!" said Blanchefleur. "Look in the closet."

In the closet, Ivan did indeed find several wooden spoons, as well as a croquet set, several pairs of boots, and a stuffed alligator.

"Beef stew," he said, tasting what was in the kettle. "Would you like some?"

"I'm quite capable of hunting for myself, thank you," said Blanchefleur. "Don't wait up. I have a feeling that when the Professor said you should be up by dawn, he meant it."

That night, Ivan slept on the second floor of the tower, where he found a bed, a desk, and a large traveling trunk with OSWALD carved on it. He wondered if Oswald had been the professor's last apprentice, the one who had been such a disappointment. In the middle of the night, he thought he felt Blanchefleur jump on the bed and curl up next to his back. But when he woke up in the morning, she was gone.

* * *

I van was used to waking up at dawn, so wake up at dawn he did. He found a small bathroom under the stairs, splashed water on his face, got dressed, and went downstairs. Blanchefleur was sitting on the table, staring at the kettle still set on it, with a look of disdain on her face.

"What is that mess?" she asked.

"I think it's pea soup," he said, after looking into the kettle. It smelled inviting, but then anything would have at that hour. Next to the kettle were a wooden bowl and spoon, as well as a napkin. "Did you put these here?" he asked Blanchefleur.

"Why would I do such a stupid thing?" she asked, and turned her back to him. She began licking her fur, as though washing herself were the most important thing in the world.

Ivan shrugged, spooned some of the pea soup into the bowl, and had a plain but filling breakfast. Afterward, he washed the bowl and spoon. As soon as he had finished eating, the kettle had emptied again—evidently, it did not need washing. Then he sat down at the table and pulled the first of Professor Owl's notes toward him.

It was tedious work. First, he would read through the notes, which were written in a cramped, slanting hand. Then, he would try to add a paragraph to the file, as neatly and succinctly as he could. He had never paid much attention in school, and writing did not come easily to him. After the first botched attempt, he learned to compose his paragraphs on the backs of Professor Owl's notes, so when he went to update the entries, he was not fumbling for words. By noon, he had finished additions to the entries on Justice, Rose, Darwin, Theosophy, Venus, Armadillo, Badminton, and Indochina. His lunch was chicken soup with noodles. He thought about having nothing but soup, every morning, noon, and night for an entire year, and longed for a sandwich.

He sat down at the table and picked up the pen, but his back and hand hurt. He put the pen down. The sunlight out the window looked so inviting. Perhaps he should go out and wander around the tower, just for a little while? Where had Blanchefleur gone, anyway? He had not seen her since breakfast. He got up, stretched, and walked out.

It had been his habit, as long as he remembered, to wander around as he wished. That was what he did now, walking around the tower and then away from it, looking idly for Blanchefleur and finding only lizards. He wandered without thinking about where he was going or how long he had been gone. The sun began to sink in the west.

That was when he realized that he had been gone for hours. Well, it would not matter, would it? He could always catch up with any work he did not finish tomorrow. He walked back in the direction of the tower, only becoming lost once. It was dark when he reached it again. He opened the door and walked in.

There were Professor Owl and Blanchefleur. The Professor was perched on the table where Ivan had been sitting earlier that day, scribbling furiously. Blanchefleur was saying, "What did you expect of someone named Idiot? I told you he would be useless."

"Oh, hello, boy," said Professor Owl, looking up. "I noticed that you went out for a walk, so I finished all of the notes for today, except Orion. I'll have that done in just a moment, and then you can sit down for dinner. I don't think I told you that each day's updates need to be filed by the end of the day, or the Encyclopedia will be incomplete. And it has never been incomplete since I started working on it, five hundred years ago."

"I'll do it," said Ivan.

"Do what?" said Blanchefleur. "Go wandering around again?"

"I'll do the update on Orion."

"That's very kind of you," said Professor Owl. "I'm sure you must be tired." But he handed Ivan the pen and hopped a bit away on the table. It was a lopsided hop: Ivan could tell that the owl's right foot was hurting. He sat and finished the update, conscious of Blanchefleur's eyes on him. When he was finished, Professor Owl read it over. "Yes, very nice," he said. "You have a clear and logical mind. Well done, boy."

Ivan looked up, startled. It was the first compliment he ever remembered receiving.

"Well, go on then, have some dinner," said Professor Owl. "And you'll be up at dawn tomorrow?"

"I'll be up at dawn," said Ivan. He knew that the next day, he would not go wandering around, at least until after the entries were finished. He did not want Blanchefleur calling him an idiot again in that tone of voice.

* * *

S ummer turned into winter. Each day, Ivan sat at the table in the tower, updating the entries for the Encyclopedia of All Knowledge. One day, he realized that he no longer needed to compose the updates on the backs of Professor Owl's notes. He could simply compose them in his head, and then write each update directly onto the file. He had not learned much in school, but he was learning now, about things that seemed useless, such as Sponge Cake, and things that seemed useful, such as Steam Engines, Epic Poetry, and Love. One morning he realized that Professor Owl had left him not only a series of updates, but also the notes for an entry on a star that had been discovered by astronomers the week before. Proudly and carefully, he took a blank file card out of the cabinet, composed a new entry for the Encyclopedia of All Knowledge, and filed the card in its place.

He came to write so well and so quickly that he would finish all of the updates, and any new entries the Professor left him, by early afternoon. After a lunch of soup, for he had never managed to get the kettle to make him anything else, however politely he asked, he would roam around the rocky countryside. Sometimes Blanchefleur would accompany him, and eventually she allowed him to carry her on his shoulder without complaining, although she was never enthusiastic. And she still called him Idiot.

One day, in February although he had lost track of the months, he updated an entry on the Trojan War. He had no idea what it was, since he had not been paying attention that day in school. So after he finished his updates, he asked the Encyclopedia. It opened to the entry on the Trojan War, which began, "It is a truth universally acknowledged that judging a beauty contest between three goddesses causes nothing but trouble." He read on, fascinated. After that day, he would spend several hours reading through whichever entries took his fancy. Each entry he read left him with more questions, and he began to wish that he could stay with Professor Owl, simply reading the entries in the Encyclopedia, forever.

But winter turned into summer, and one day the professor said, "Ivan, it has been a year since you arrived, and the term of your apprenticeship with me is at an end. Thank you for all of the care and attention you have put into your task. As a reward, I will give you one of my feathers—that one right there. Pluck it out gently. *Gently!*"

Ivan held up the feather. It was long and straight, with brown and white stripes.

"Cut the end of it with a penknife and make it into a pen," said Professor Owl. "If you ever want to access the Encyclopedia, just tell the pen what you would like to know, and it will write the entry for you."

"Thank you," said Ivan. "But couldn't I stay—"

"Of course not," said Blanchefleur. "My mother is expecting us. So come on already." And indeed, since it was dawn, Professor Owl was already heading up the stairs, for he had very important things to do during the day. Owls do, you know.

The Castle in the Forest looked just as Ivan remembered. There were cats tending the gardens, where the roses were once again blooming, as though they had never stopped. Marmalade greeted them at the door and led them to the Lady's solar, where she was sitting at a desk, writing. Her cats-in-waiting were embroidering a tapestry, and one was strumming a lute with her claws, playing a melody Ivan remembered from when he was a child.

"Well?" she said when she looked up. "How did Ivan do, my dear?"

"Well enough," said Blanchefleur. "Are there any mouse pies? We've been walking all day, and I'm hungry."

Really it had been Ivan who had been walking all day. He had carried Blanchefleur most of the way, except when she wanted to drink from a puddle or play with a leaf.

"Wait until the banquet," said the Lady. "It starts in an hour, which will give you enough time to prepare. It's in honor of your return and departure."

"Departure?" said Ivan.

"Yes," said the Lady. "Tomorrow, you will go to the Southern Marshes, to spend a year with my friend, Dame Lizard. She has a large family, and needs help taking care of it. Blanchefleur, you will accompany your cousin."

"But that's not fair!" said Blanchefleur. "I've already spent a year with Ivan Idiot. Why do I have to spend another year with him?"

"Because he is your cousin, and he needs your help," said the Lady. "Now go, the both of you. I don't think you realize quite how dirty you both are." And she was right. From the long journey, even Blanchefleur's white paws were covered with dirt.

As they walked upstairs, Ivan said, "I'm sorry you have to come with me, Blanchefleur. I know you dislike being with me."

"You're not so bad," she said grudgingly. "At least you're warm." So it had been her, sleeping against his back all those nights. Ivan was surprised and pleased at the thought.

That night, the banquet proceeded as it had the year before, except this time Ivan knew what to expect. Several of the female cats asked him to dance, and this time he danced with more skill, never once stepping on a cat paw or tail. He danced several times with Blanchefleur, and she did not seem to dislike it as much as she had last year. Tailcatcher, the striped cat, was there as well. Once, as they were dancing close to one another, Ivan heard a hiss, but when he turned to look at Tailcatcher, the cat was bowing to his partner.

At the end of the evening, as he wearily climbed the stone stairs up to his bed, he passed a hallway and heard a murmur of voices. At the end of the hallway stood Tailcatcher and Blanchefleur. He spoke to her and she replied, too low for Ivan to hear what they were saying. Then she turned and walked on down the hallway, her tail held high, exactly the way she walked when she was displeased with him. Ivan was rather glad that Tailcatcher had been rebuffed, whatever he had wanted from her.

As he sank into sleep that night in the curtained bed, he wondered if she would come to curl up against his back. But he fell asleep too quickly to find out.

The next morning, they started for the Southern Marshes. As they traveled south, the forest grew less dense: the trees were sparser, more sunlight fell on the path, and soon Ivan was hot and sweating. At midafternoon, they came to a river, and he was able to swim and cool himself off. Blanchefleur refused to go anywhere near the water.

"I'm not a fish," she said. "Are you quite done? We still have a long way to go."

Ivan splashed around a bit more, then got out and dried himself as best he could. They followed the river south until it was no longer a river but a series of creeks running through low hills covered with willows, alders, and sycamores. Around the creeks grew cattails, and where the water formed into pools, he could see waterlilies starting to bloom. They were constantly crossing water, so Ivan carried Blanchefleur, who did not like to get her feet wet.

"There," she said finally. "That's where we're going." She was pointing at one of the low hills. At first, Ivan did not see the stone house among the trees: it blended in so well with the gray trunks. Ivan walked through a narrow creek (he had long ago given up on keeping his shoes dry) and up the hill to the house. He knocked at the door.

From inside, he heard a crash, then a "Just a moment!" Then another crash and the voice yelling, "Get out of there at once, Number Seven!"

There were more crashes and bangs, and then the door opened, so abruptly that he stepped back, startled. He might have been startled anyway, because who should be standing in front of him but a lizard, who came almost up to his shoulders, in a long brown duster and a feathered hat askew over one ear.

"I'm so glad you're here!" she said. "They've been impossible today. But they are dears, really they are, and the Lady told me that you were a competent nursemaid. You are competent, aren't you?" Without waiting for a reply, she continued, "Oh, it's good to see you again, Blanchefleur. Did you like the shrunken head I sent you from Peru?"

"Not particularly," said the white cat.

"Splendid!" said the lizard. "Now I'll just be off, shall I? My train leaves in half an hour and I don't want to miss it. I'm going to Timbuktu, you know. Train and then boat and train again, then camel caravan. Doesn't that sound fun? Do help me get my suitcases on the bicycle."

The bicycle was in a sort of shed. Ivan helped her tie two suitcases onto a rack with some frayed rope that he hoped would hold all the way to the station.

"Such a handy one, your young man, my dear," said the lizard to Blanchefleur.

"He's not—" said Blanchefleur.

"Kisses to you both! Ta, and I'll see you in a year! If I survive the sands of the Sahara, of course." And then she was off on her bicycle, down a road that ran across the hills, with her hat still askew. As she rode out of sight, Ivan heard a faint cry: "Plenty of spiders, that's what they like! And don't let them stay up too late!"

"Don't let who stay up too late?" asked Ivan.

"Us!" Ivan turned around. There in the doorway stood five—no, six—no, seven lizards that came up to his knees.

"Who are you?" he asked.

"These are her children," said Blanchefleur. "You're supposed to take care of them while she's gone. Don't you know who she is? She's Emilia Lizard, the travel writer. And you're her nursemaid." Blanchefleur seemed amused at the prospect.

"But the Lady said I was supposed to help," said Ivan. "How can I help someone who's on her way to Timbuktu? I don't know anything about taking care of children—or lizards!"

"It's easy," said one of the lizards. "You just let us do anything we want!"

"Eat sweets," said another.

"Stay up late," said yet another.

"Play as long as we like," said either one who had already spoken or another one, it was difficult to tell because they kept weaving in and out of the group, and they all looked alike.

"Please stand still," he said. "You're giving me a headache. And tell me your names."

"We don't have names," said one. "Mother just calls us by numbers, but she always gets us mixed up."

"I'll have to give you names," said Ivan, although he was afraid that he would get them mixed up as well. "Let's at least go in. Blanchefleur and I are tired, and we need to rest."

But once they stepped inside, Ivan found there was no place to rest. All of the furniture in the parlor had been piled in a corner to make a fort.

"If I'm going to take care of you, I need to learn about you," said Ivan. "Let's sit down—" But there was nowhere to sit down. And the lizards, all seven of them, were no longer there. Some were already inside the fort, and the others were about to besiege it.

"Come out!" he said. "Come out, all of you!" But his voice was drowned by the din they were already making. "What in the world am I supposed to do?" he asked Blanchefleur.

She twitched her tail, then said in a low voice, "I think it's the Seige of Jerusalem." Loudly and theatrically, she said, as though to Ivan, "Yes, you're right. The French are so much better at cleaning than the Saracens. I bet the French would clean up this mess lickety split."

Ivan stared at her in astonishment. Then he smiled. "You're wrong, Blanchefleur. The Saracens have a long tradition of cleanliness. In a cleaning contest, the Saracens would certainly win."

"Would not!" said one of the besiegers. "Would too!" came a cry from the fort. And then, in what seemed like a whirlwind of lizards, the fort was disassembled, the sofa and armchairs were put back in their places, and even the cushions were fluffed. In front of Ivan stood a line of seven lizards, asking "Who won, who won?"

"The Saracens, this time," said Blanchefleur. "But really, you know, it's two out of three that counts."

Life in the Lizard household was completely different than it had been in Professor Owl's tower. There were days when Ivan missed the silence and solitude, the opportunity to read and study all day long. But he did not have much time to remember or regret. His days were spent catching insects and spiders for the lizards' breakfast, lunch, snack, and dinner, making sure that they bathed and sunned themselves, that they napped in the afternoon and went to bed on time.

At first, it was difficult to make them pay attention. They were as quick as seven winks, and on their outings they had a tendency to vanish as soon as he turned his back. Ivan was always afraid he was going to lose one. Once, indeed, he had to rescue Number Two from an eagle, and Number Five had to be pulled out of a fox hole. But he found that the hours spent working on the Encyclopedia of All Knowledge stood him in good stead: if he began telling a story, in an instant they would all be seated around him, listening intently. And if he forgot anything, he would ask the pen he had made from Professor Owl's tail feather to write it out for him. Luckily, Dame Lizard had left plenty of paper and ink.

He gave them all names: Ajax, Achilles, Hercules, Perseus, Helen, Medea, Andromache. They were fascinated by the stories of their names, and Medea insisted that she was putting spells on the others, while Hercules would try to lift the heaviest objects he could find. Ivan learned to tell them apart. One had an ear that was slightly crooked, one had a stubby tail, one swayed as she walked. Each night, when he tucked them in and counted the lizard heads—yes, seven heads lay on the pillows—he breathed a sigh of relief that they were still alive.

"How many more days?" he would ask Blanchefleur.

"You don't want to know," she would reply. And then she would go out hunting, while he made himself dinner. Of course he could not eat insects and spiders, or mice like Blanchefleur. On the first night, he looked in the pantry and found a bag of flour, a bag of sugar, some tea, and a tinned ham. He made himself tea and ate part of the tinned ham.

"What in the world shall I do for food?" he asked Blanchefleur.

"What everyone else does. Work for it," she replied. So the next day, he left the lizards in her care for a couple of hours and went into the town that lay along the road Dame Lizard had taken. It was a small town, not much larger than the village he had grown up in. There, he asked if anyone needed firewood chopped, or a field cleared, or any such work. That day, he cleaned out a pigsty. The farmer who hired him found him strong and steady, so he hired him again, to pick vegetables, paint a fence, any odd work that comes up around a farm. He recommended Ivan to others, so there was soon a steady trickle of odd jobs that brought in enough money for him to buy bread and meat. The farmer who had originally hired him gave him vegetables that were too ripe for market.

He could never be gone long, because Blanchfleur would remind him in no uncertain terms that taking care of the lizards was his task, not hers. Whenever he came back, they were clean and fed and doing something orderly, like playing board games.

"Why do they obey you, and not me?" he asked, tired and cross. He had just washed an entire family's laundry.

"Because," she answered.

After dinner, once the lizards had been put to bed, really and finally put to bed, he would sit in the parlor and read the books on the shelves, which were all about travel in distant lands. Among them were the books of Dame Emilia Lizard. They had titles like *Up the Amazon in a Steamboat* and *Across the Himalayas on a Yak*. He found them interesting—Dame Lizard was an acute observer, and he learned about countries and customs that he had not even known existed—but often he could scarcely keep his eyes open because he was so tired. Once Blanchefleur returned from her evening hunt, he would go to sleep in Dame Lizard's room. He could tell it was hers because the walls were covered with photographs of her in front of temples and pyramids, perched on yaks or camels or water buffalos, dressed in native garb. Blanchefleur would curl up against him, no longer pretending not to, and he would fall asleep to her soft rumble.

In winter, all the lizards caught bronchitis. First Andromache started coughing, and then Ajax, until there was an entire household of sick lizards. Since Ivan did not want to leave them, Blanchefleur went into town to find the doctor.

"You're lucky to have caught me," said the doctor when he arrived. "My train leaves in an hour. There's been a dragon attack, and the King has asked all the medical personnel who can be spared to help the victims. He burned an entire village, can you imagine? But I'm sure you've seen the photographs in the *Herald*."

Ivan had not—they did not get the *Herald*, or any other newspaper, at Dame Lizard's house. He asked where the attack had occurred, and sighed with relief when told it was a fishing village on the coast. His father was not in danger.

"Nothing much I can do here anyway," said the doctor. "Bronchitis has to run its course. Give them tea with honey for the coughs, and tepid baths for the fever. And try to avoid catching it yourself!"

"A dragon attack," said Blanchefleur after the doctor had left. "We haven't had one of those in a century."

But there was little time to think of what might be happening far away. For weeks, Ivan barely slept. He told the lizards stories, took their temperature, made them tea. Once their appetites returned, he found them the juiciest worms under the snow. Slowly, one by one, they began to get better. Medea, the smallest of them and his secret favorite, was sick for longer than the rest, and one night when she was coughing badly, he held her through the night, not knowing what else to do. Sometimes, when he looked as though he might fall asleep standing up, Blanchefleur would say, "Go sleep, Ivan. I'll stay up and watch them. I am nocturnal, you know."

By the time all the lizards were well, the marsh marigolds were blooming, and irises were pushing their sword-like leaves out of the ground. The marshes were filled with the sounds of birds returning from the south: the raucous cacophony of ducks, the songs of thrushes.

Ivan had forgotten how long he had been in the marsh, so he was startled when one morning he heard the front door open and a voice call, "Hello, my dears! I'm home!" And there stood Dame Lizard, with her suitcases strapped to her bicycle, looking just as she had left a year ago, but with a fuschia scarf around her throat.

The lizards rushed around her, calling "Mother, Mother, look how we've grown! We all have names now! And we know about the Trojan War!" She had brought them a set of papier-mâché puppets and necklaces of lapis lazuli. For Blanchefleur, she had brought a hat of crimson felt that she had seen on a dancing monkey in Marakesh. Blanchefleur said, "Thank you. You shouldn't have."

Once the presents were distributed and the lizards were eating an enormous box of Turkish Delight, she said to Ivan, "Come outside." When they were standing by the house, under the alders, she said, "Ivan, I can see you've taken good care of my children. They are happy and healthy, and that is due to your dedication. Hercules told me how you took care of Medea when she was ill. I want to give you a present too. I brought back a camel whip for you, but I want to give you something that will be of more use, since you don't have a camel. You must raise your arms, then close your eyes and stand as still as possible, no matter how startled you may be."

Ivan closed his eyes, not knowing what to expect.

And then he felt a terrible constriction around his chest, as though his ribcage were being crushed. He opened his eyes, looked down, and gasped.

There, wrapped around his chest, was what looked like a thick green rope. It was Dame Lizard's tail, which had been hidden under her skirt. For a moment, the tail tightened, and then it was no longer attached to her body. She had shed it, as lizards do. Ivan almost fell forward from the relief of being able to breathe.

"I learned that from a Swami in India," she said. "From now on, when you give pain to another, you will feel my tail tightening around you so whatever pain you give, you will also receive. That's called empathy, and the Swami said it was the most important thing anyone can have."

Ivan looked down. He could no longer see the tail, but he could feel it around him, like a band under his shirt. He did not know whether to thank her. The gift, if gift it was, had been so painful that he felt sore and bruised.

After he had said a protracted farewell to all the lizards, hugging them tightly, he and Blanchefleur walked north, along the river. He told her what Dame Lizard had done, lifting his shirt and showing her the mark he had found there, like a tattoo of a green tail around his ribcage.

"Is it truly a gift, or a curse?" he asked Blanchefleur.

"One never knows about gifts until later," said the white cat.

* * *

M armalade met them at the front door. "I'm so sorry, Miss
Blanchefleur," he said, "but your mother is not home. The
King has asked her to the castle, to consult about the dragon attack.
But she left you a note in the solar."

Blanchefleur read the note to Ivan.

*My dear, Ivan's third apprenticeship is with Captain Wolf in the
Northern Mountains. Could you please accompany him and try to keep
him from getting killed? Love, Mother*

This time, there was no banquet. With the Lady gone, the castle
was quiet, as though it were asleep and waiting for her return to wake
back up. They ate dinner in the kitchen with Mrs. Pebbles and the
ladies-in-waiting, and then went directly to bed. Blanchefleur curled
up next to Ivan on the pillow, as usual. It had become their custom.

The next morning, Mrs. Pebbles gave them Ivan's satchel, with
clean clothes, including some warmer ones for the mountains, and
his horn-handled knife. "Take care of each other," she told them.
"Those mountains aren't safe, and I don't know what the Lady is
thinking, sending you to the Wolf Guard."

"What is the Wolf Guard?" Ivan asked as they walked down the
garden path.

"It's part of the King's army," said Blanchefleur. "It guards the
northern borders from trolls. They come down from the mountains
and raid the towns. In winter, especially . . ."

"Blanchefleur!" Tailcatcher was standing in front of them. He
had stepped out from behind one of the topiaries. "May I have a
word with you?" He did not, however, sound as though he were
asking permission. Ivan gritted his teeth. He had never spoken to
Blanchefleur like that—even if he had wanted to, he would not have
dared.

"Yes, and the word is no," said Blanchefleur. She walked right
around him, holding her tail high, and Ivan followed her, making a
wide circle around the striped cat, who looked as though he might
take a swipe at Ivan's shins. He looked back, to see Tailcatcher glaring
at them.

"What was that about?" asked Ivan.

"For years now, he's been assuming I would marry him, because
he's the best hunter in the castle. He asked me the first time on the
night before we left for Professor Owl's house, and then again before
we left for Dame Lizard's. This would have been the third time."

"And you keep refusing?" asked Ivan.

"Of course," she said. "He may be the best hunter, but I'm the daughter of the Lady of the Forest and the Man in the Moon. I'm not going to marry a common cat!"

Ivan could not decide how he felt about her response. On the one hand, he was glad she had no intention of marrying Tailcatcher. On the other, wasn't he a common man?

This journey was longer and harder than the two before. Once they reached the foothills of the Northern Mountains, they were constantly going up. The air was colder. In late afternoon, Ivan put on a coat that Mrs. Pebbles had insisted on packing for him, and that he had been certain he would not need until winter.

Eventually, there were no more roads or paths, and they simply walked through the forest. Ivan started wondering whether Blanchefleur knew the way, then scolded himself. Of course she did: she was Blanchefleur.

Finally, as the sun was setting, Blanchefleur said, "We're here."

"Where?" asked Ivan. They were standing in a clearing. Around them were tall pines. Ahead of them was what looked like a sheer cliff face, rising higher than the treetops. Above it, he could see the peaks of the mountains, glowing in the light of the setting sun.

Blanchefleur jumped down from his shoulder, walked over to a boulder in the middle of the clearing, and climbed to the top. She said, "Captain, we have arrived."

Out of the shadows of the forest appeared wolves, as silently as though they were shadows themselves—Ivan could not count how many. They were all around, and he suddenly realized that he could die, here in the forest. He imagined their teeth at his throat and turned to run, then realized that he was being an idiot, giving in to an ancient instinct although he could see that Blanchefleur was not frightened at all. She sat on the dark rock, amid the dark wolves, like a ghost.

"Greetings, Blanchefleur," said one of the wolves, distinguishable from the others because he had only one eye, and a scar running across it from his ear to his muzzle. "I hear that your mother has sent us a new recruit."

"For a year," said Blanchefleur. "Try not to get him killed."

"I make no promises," said the wolf. "What is his name?"

"Ivan," said Blanchefleur.

"Come here, recruit." Ivan walked to the boulder and stood in front of the wolf, as still as he could. He did not want Blanchefleur to see that he was afraid. "You shall call me Captain, and I shall call you Private, and as long as you do exactly as you are told, all shall be well between us. Do you understand?"

"Yes," said Ivan.

The wolf bared his teeth and growled.

"Yes, Captain," said Ivan.

"Good. This is your Company, although we like to think of ourselves as a pack. You are a member of the Wolf Guard, and should be prepared to die for your brothers and sisters of the pack, as they are prepared to die for you. Now come inside."

Ivan wondered where inside might be, but the Captain loped toward the cliff face and vanished behind an outcropping. One by one, the wolves followed him, some stopping to give Ivan a brief sniff. Ivan followed them and realized that the cliff was not sheer after all. Behind a protruding rock was a narrow opening, just large enough for a wolf. He crawled through it and emerged in a large cave. Scattered around the cave, wolves were sitting or lying in groups, speaking together in low voices. They looked up when he entered, but were too polite or uninterested to stare and went back to their conversations, which seemed to be about troll raiding parties they had encountered, wounds they had sustained, and the weather.

"Have you ever fought?" the Captain asked him.

"No, sir," said Ivan.

"That is bad," said the Captain. "Can you move through the forest silently? Can you tell your direction from the sun in the day and the stars at night? Can you sound like an owl to give warning without divulging your presence?"

"Yes, Captain," said Ivan, fairly certain that he could still do those things. And to prove it to himself, he hooted, first like a Eagle Owl, then like a Barn Owl, and finally like one of the Little Owls that used to nest in his father's mill.

"Well, that's something, at least. You can be one of our scouts. Have you eaten?"

"No, sir," said Ivan.

"At the back of the cave are the rabbits we caught this morning," said the Captain. "You may have one of those."

"He is human," said Blanchefleur. "He must cook his food."

"A nuisance, but you may build a small fire, although you will have to collect wood. These caverns extend into the mountain for several miles. Make certain the smoke goes back into the mountain, and not through the entrance."

Skinning a rabbit was messy work, but Ivan butchered it, giving a leg to Blanchefleur and roasting the rest for himself on a stick he sharpened with his knife. It was better than he had expected. That night, he slept beneath his coat on the floor of the cave, surrounded by wolves. He was grateful to have Blanchefleur curled up next to his chest.

The next morning, he began his life in the Wolf Guard.

As a scout, his duty was not to engage the trolls, but to look for signs of them. He would go out with a wolf partner, moving through the forest silently, looking for signs of troll activity: their camps, their tracks, their spoor. The Wolf Guard kept detailed information on the trolls who lived in the mountains. In summer, they seldom came down far enough to threaten the villages on the slopes. But in winter, they would send raiding parties for all the things they could not produce themselves: bread and cheese and beer, fabrics and jewels, sometimes even children they could raise as their own, for troll women do not bear many children. Ivan learned the forest quickly, just as he had at home, and the wolves in his Company, who had initially been politely contemptuous of a human in their midst, came to think of him as a useful member of the pack. He could not smell as well as they could, nor see as well at night, but he could climb trees, and pull splinters out of their paws, and soon he was as good at tracking the trolls as they were. They were always respectful to Blanchefleur. One day, he asked her what she did while he was out with the wolves. "Mind my own business," she said. So he did not ask again.

As for Ivan, being a scout in the Wolf Guard was like finding a home. He had learned so much in Professor Owl's tower, and he had come to love the lizards in his charge, but with the wolves he was back in the forest, where he had spent his childhood. And the wolves themselves were like a family. When Graypaw or Mist, with whom he was most often paired, praised his ability to spot troll tracks, or when the Captain said "Well done, Private," he felt a pride that he had never felt before.

"You know, I don't think I've ever seen you so happy," said Blanchefleur, one winter morning. The snows had come, and he was grateful for the hat and gloves that Mrs. Pebbles had included in his satchel.

"I don't think I ever have been, before," he said. "Not since—" Since his mother had died. Since then, he had always been alone. But now he had a pack. "I think I could stay here for the rest of my life."

"We seldom get what we want," said Blanchefleur. "The world has a use for us, tasks we must fulfill. And we must fulfill them as best we can, finding happiness along the way. But we usually get what we need."

"I've never heard you so solemn before," said Ivan. "You're starting to sound like your mother. But I don't think the world has any tasks for me. I'm no one special, after all."

"Don't be so sure, Ivan Miller," said Blanchefleur.

Suddenly, all the wolves in the cave pricked up their ears.

"The signal!" said the Captian.

And then Ivan heard it too, the long howl that signaled a troll raid, the short howls that indicated which village was being attacked.

"To the village!" shouted the Captain.

"Be careful!" said Blanchefleur, as Ivan sprang up, made sure his knife was in his belt, and ran out of the cave with the wolves. Then they were coursing through the forest, silent shadows against the snow.

They saw the flames and heard the screams before they saw any trolls. The village was a small one, just a group of herding families on the upper slopes. Their houses were simple, made of stone, with turf roofs. But the sheds were of wood, filled with fodder for the sturdy mountain sheep. The trolls had set fire to the fodder, and some of the sheds were burning. The sheep were bleating terribly, and as wolves rushed into the village, the Captain shouted to Ivan, "Open the pens! Let the sheep out—we can herd them back later."

Ivan ran from pen to pen, opening all the gates. Mist ran beside him and if any sheep were reluctant to leave their pens, she herded them out, nipping at their heels.

When they reached the last of the pens, Ivan saw his first troll. She was taller than the tallest man, and twice as large around. She looked like a piece of the mountain that had grown arms and legs.

Her mottled skin was gray and green and brown, and she was covered in animal pelts. In her hand, she carried a large club. In front of her, crouched and growling, was Graypaw.

"Come on, cub!" she sneered "I'll teach you how to sit and lie down!"

She lunged at Graypaw, swinging the club clumsily but effectively. The club hit a panicked ram that had been standing behind her, and the next moment, the ram lay dead on the snow.

Mist yipped to let Graypaw know she was behind him. He barked back, and the wolves circled the troll in opposite directions, one attacking from the left and the other from the right.

What could Ivan do? He drew his knife, but that would be no more effective against a troll than a sewing needle. To his right, one of the sheds was on fire, pieces of it falling to the ground as it burned. As Graypaw and Mist circled, keeping away from the club, trying to get under it and bite the troll's ankles, Ivan ran into the burning shed. He wrenched a piece of wood from what had been a gate, but was now in flames, then thrust its end into the fire. The flames licked it, and it caught. A long stick, its end on fire. This was a weapon of sorts, but how was he to use it?

Graypaw and Mist were still circling, and one of them had succeeded in wounding the troll—there was green ichor running down her leg. The troll was paying no attention to Ivan—she was wholly absorbed in fending off the wolves. But the wolves knew he was behind them. They were watching him out of the corners of their eyes, waiting. For what?

Then Ivan gave a short bark, the signal for attack. Both Graypaw and Mist flew at the troll simultaneously. The troll swung about wildly, not certain which to dispatch first. *Now*, thought Ivan, and he lunged forward, not caring that he could be hit by the club, only knowing this was the moment, that he had put his packmates in danger for this opportunity. He thrust the flaming stick toward the troll's face. The troll shrieked—it had gone straight into her left eye. She clutched the eye and fell backward. Without thinking, Ivan drew his knife and plunged it into the troll's heart, or where he thought her heart might be.

A searing pain ran through his chest. It was Dame Lizard's tail, tightening until he could no longer breathe. It loosened again, but he reeled with the shock and pain of it.

"Ivan, are you well?" asked Mist.

"I'm—all right," he said, still breathless. "I'm going to be all right." But he felt sick.

The troll lay on the ground, green ichor spreading across her chest. She was dead. Behind her was a large sack.

"That must be what she was stealing," said Graypaw.

The sack started to wriggle.

"A sheep, perhaps," said Mist.

But when Ivan untied it, he saw a dirty, frightened face, with large gray eyes. A girl.

"You've found my daughter!" A woman was running toward them. With her was the Captain.

"Nadia, my Nadia," she cried.

"Mama!" cried the girl, and scrambling out of the bag, she ran into her mother's arms.

"This is the Mayor of the village," said the Captain. "Most of the trolls have fled, and we were afraid they had taken the girl with them."

"I can't thank you enough," said the woman. "You've done more than rescue my daughter, although that has earned you my gratitude. I recognize this troll—she has been here before. We call her Old Mossy. She is the leader of this tribe, and without her, the tribe will need to choose a new leader by combat. It will not come again this winter. Our village has sustained great damage, but not one of us has died or disappeared, and we can rebuild. How can we reward you for coming to our rescue, Captain?"

"Madame Mayor, we are the Wolf Guard. Your gratitude is our reward," said the Captain.

On the way back to the cave, Graypaw and Mist walked ahead of Ivan, talking to the Captain in low voices. He wondered if he had done something wrong. Perhaps he should not have told them to attack? After all, they both outranked him. They were both Corporals, while he was only a Private. Perhaps they were telling the Captain about how he had reeled and clutched his chest after the attack. Would he be declared unfit for combat?

When they got back to the cave, Blanchefleur was waiting for him.

"Ivan, I need to speak with you," she said.

"Blanchefleur, I killed a troll! I mean, I helped kill her. I want to tell you about it . . ."

"That's wonderful, Ivan. I'm very proud of you. I am, you know, and not just because of the troll. But it's time for us to leave."

"What do you mean? It's still winter. I haven't been here for a year yet."

"My mother has summoned us. Here is her messenger."

It was Tailcatcher. In his excitement, Ivan had not noticed the striped cat.

"The Lady wishes you to travel to the capital. Immediately," said Tailcatcher.

"But why?" asked Ivan.

"You are summoned," said Tailcatcher, contemptuously. "Is that not enough?"

"If you are summoned, you must go," said the Captain, who had been standing behind him. "But come back to us when you can, Ivan."

Ivan had never felt so miserable in his life. "Can I say goodbye to Mist and Graypaw?"

"Yes, quickly," said the Captain. "And thank them, because on their recommendation, I am promoting you to Corporal. There is also something I wish to give you. Hold out your right hand, Corporal Miller."

Ivan held out his hand.

The Captain lunged at him, seized Ivan's hand in his great mouth, and bit down.

Ivan cried out.

The Captain released him. The wolf's teeth had not broken his skin, but one of his fangs had pierced Ivan's hand between the thumb and forefinger. It was still lodged in his flesh. There was no blood, and as Ivan watched, the fang vanished, leaving only a white fang-shaped scar.

"Why—" he asked.

"That is my gift to you, Corporal. When I was a young corporal like yourself, I saved the life of a witch. In return, she charmed that fang for me. She told me that as long as I had it, whenever I fought, I would defeat my enemy. She also told me that one day, I could pass the charm to another. I asked her how, and she told me I would know when the time came. I am old, Ivan, and this is my last winter with the Wolf Guard. I believe I know why you have been summoned by the Lady. With that charm, whatever battles you have to fight, you should win. Now go. There is a storm coming, and you should be off the mountain before it arrives."

Ivan packed his belongings and made his farewells. Then, he left the cave, following Tailcatcher and Blanchefleur. He looked back once, with tears in his eyes, and felt as though his heart were breaking.

The journey to the capital would have taken several days, but in the first town they came to, Ivan traded his knife and coat for a horse. It was an old farm horse, but it went faster than he could have on foot with two cats. The cats sat in panniers that had once held potatoes, and Tailcatcher looked very cross indeed. When Ivan asked again why he had been summoned, the cat replied, "That's for the Lady to say," and would say nothing more.

They spent the night in a barn and arrived at the capital the next day.

Ivan had never seen a city so large. The houses had as many as three stories, and there were shops for everything, from ladies' hats and fancy meats to bicycles. On one street he even saw a shiny new motorcar. But where were the people? The shops were closed, the houses shuttered, and the streets empty. Once, he saw a frightened face peering at him out of an alley, before it disappeared into the shadows.

"What happened here?" he asked.

"You'll know soon enough," said Tailcather. "That's where we're going."

That was the palace.

Ivan had never seen a building so large. His father's mill could have fit into one of its towers. With a sense of unease, he rode up to the gates.

"State your business!" said a guard who had been crouching in the gatehouse and stood up only long enough to challenge them.

Ivan was about to reply when Blanchefleur poked her head out of the pannier. "I am Blanchefleur. My mother is the Lady of the Forest, and our business is our own."

"You may pass, My Lady," said the guard, hurriedly opening the gates and then hiding again.

They rode up the long avenue, through the palace gardens, which were magnificent, although Ivan thought they were not as interesting as the Lady's gardens with their cat gardeners. They left the horse with an ostler who met them at the palace steps, then hurried off toward the stables. At the top of the steps, they were met by a majordomo who said, "This way, this way." He reminded Ivan of Marmalade.

They followed the majordomo down long hallways with crimson carpets and paintings on the walls in gilded frames. At last, they came to a pair of gilded doors, which opened into the throne room. There was the King, seated on his throne. Ivan could tell he was the King because he wore a crown. To one side of him sat the Lady. To the other sat a girl about Ivan's age, also wearing a crown, and with a scowl on her face. Before the dais stood two men.

"Ivan," said the Lady, "I'm so pleased to see you. I'm afraid we have a problem on our hands. About a year ago, a dragon arrived on the coast. At first, he only attacked the ports and coastal villages, and then only occasionally. I believe he is a young dragon, and lacked confidence in his abilities. But several months ago, he started flying inland, attacking market towns. Last week, he was spotted in the skies over the capital, and several days ago, he landed on the central bank. That's where he is now, holed up in the vault. Dragons like gold, as you know. The King has asked for a dragon slayer, and I'm hoping you'll volunteer."

"What?" said Ivan. "The King has asked for a what?"

"Yes, young man," said the King, looking annoyed that the Lady had spoken first. "We've already tried to send the municipal police after him, only to have the municipal police eaten. The militias were not able to stop him in the towns, but I thought that a trained police force—well, that's neither here nor there. The Lady tells me that a dragon must be slain in the old-fashioned way. I'm a progressive man myself—this entire city should be wired for electricity by next year, assuming it's not destroyed by the dragon. But with a dragon sitting on the monetary supply, I'm willing to try anything. So we've made the usual offer: the hand of my daughter in marriage and the kingdom after I retire, which should be in about a decade, barring ill health. We already have two brave volunteers, Sir Albert Anglethorpe and Oswald the—what did you say it was? the Omnipotent."

Sir Albert, a stocky man with a shock of blonde hair, bowed. He was wearing chain mail and looked as though he exercised regularly with kettlebells. Oswald the Omnipotent, a tall, thin, pimply man in a ratty robe, said "How de do."

"And you are?" said the King.

"Corporal Miller," said Ivan. "And I have no idea how to slay a dragon."

"Honesty! I like honesty," said the King. "None of us do either. But you'll figure it out, won't you, Corporal Miller? Because the dragon really must be slain, and I'm at my wits' end. The city evacuated, no money to pay the military—we won't be a proper kingdom if this keeps up."

"I have every confidence in you, Ivan," said the Lady.

"Me too," said Blanchefleur.

Startled, Ivan looked down at the white cat. "May I have something to eat before I go, um, dragon-slaying?" he asked. "We've been traveling all morning."

"Of course," said the King. "Anything you want, my boy. Ask and it will be yours."

"Well then," said Ivan, "I'd like some paper and ink."

Sir Albert had insisted on being fully armed, so he wore a suit of armor and carried a sword and shield. Oswald was still in his ratty robe and carried what he said was a magic wand.

"A witch sold it to me," he told Ivan. "It can transform anything it touches into anything else. She told me it had two transformations left it in. I used the first one to turn a rock into a sack of gold, but I lost the gold in a card game. So when I heard about this dragon, I figured I would use the second transformation to turn him into—I don't know, maybe a frog? And then, I'll be king. They give you all the gold you want, when you're king."

"What about the princess?" asked Ivan.

"Oh, she's pretty enough. Although she looks bad-tempered."

"And do you want to be king too?" Ivan asked Sir Albert.

"What? I don't care about that," he said through the visor of his helmet. "It's the dragon I'm after. I've been the King's champion three years running. I can out-joust and out-fight any man in the kingdom. But can I slay a dragon, eh? That's what I want to know." He bent his arms as though he were flexing his biceps, although they were hidden in his armor.

Ivan had not put on armor, but he had asked for a bow and a quiver of arrows. They seemed inadequate, compared with a sword and a magic wand.

The dragon may have been young, but he was not small. Ivan, Oswald, and Sir Alfred stood in front of the bank building, looking at the damage he had caused. There was a large hole in the side of the building where he had smashed through the stone wall, directly into the vault.

"As the King's champion, I insist that I be allowed to fight the dragon first," said Sir Albert. "Also, I outrank both of you."

"Fine by me," said Oswald.

"All right," said Ivan.

Sir Albert clanked up the front steps and through the main entrance. They heard a roar, and then a crash, as though a file cabinet had fallen over, and then nothing.

After fifteen mintues, Oswald asked, "So how big do you think this dragon is, anyway?"

"About as big as the hole in the side of the building," said Ivan.

"See, the reason I'm asking," said Oswald, "is that the wand has to actually touch whatever I want to transform. Am I going to be able to touch the dragon without being eaten?"

"Probably not," said Ivan. "They breathe fire, you know."

"What about when they're sleeping?" asked Oswald.

"Dragons are very light sleepers," said Ivan. "He would smell you before you got close enough."

"How do you know?"

"It's in the Encyclopedia of All Knowledge."

"Oh, that thing," said Oswald. "You know, I worked on that for a while. Worst job I ever had. The pay was terrible, and I had to eat soup for every meal."

Another half hour passed.

"I don't think Sir Albert is coming out," said Ivan. "You volunteered before me. Would you like to go next?"

"You know, I'm not so sure about going in after all," said Oswald. "I can't very well rule a kingdom if I'm eaten, can I?"

"That might be difficult," said Ivan.

"You go ahead," said Oswald, starting to back away. "I think I'm going to turn another rock into gold coins. That seems like a better idea."

He turned and ran up the street, leaving Ivan alone in front of the bank. Ivan sighed. Well, there was no reason to wait any longer. He might as well go in now.

Instead of going in by the front door, he went in through the hole that the dragon had made in the side of the bank. He walked noiselessly, as he had done in the forest. It was easy to find the dragon: he was lying on a pile of gold coins in the great stone room that had once been the vault. Near the door of the vault, which had been smashed open, Ivan could see a suit of armor and a sword, blackened by flames. He did not want to think about what had happened to Sir Albert.

An arrow would not penetrate the dragon's hide. He knew that, because while he had been eating at the palace, he had asked Professor Owl's tail feather to write out the entire Encyclopedia entry on dragons. He had a plan, and would get only one chance to carry it out. It would depend as much on luck as skill.

But even if it worked, he knew how it would feel, slaying a dragon. He remembered how it had felt, killing the troll. Could he survive the pain? Was there any way to avoid it? He had to try.

He stood in a narrow hallway off the vault. Keeping back in the shadows, he called, "Dragon!"

The dragon lifted his head. "Another dragon slayer? How considerate of the King to sent me dessert! Dragon slayer is my favorite delicacy, although the policemen were delicious. I much preferred them to farmers, who taste like dirt and leave grit between your teeth, or fishermen, who are too salty."

"Dragon, you could fly north to the mountains. There are plenty of sheep to eat there."

"Sheep!" said the dragon. "Sheep are dull and stringy compared to the delicious men I've eaten here. Just the other day, I ate a fat baker. He tasted of sugar and cinnamon. There are plenty of teachers and accountants to eat in this city. Why, I might eat the Princess herself! I hear princess is even better than dragon slayer."

The dragon swung his head around, as though trying to locate Ivan. "But you don't smell like a man, dragon slayer," said the dragon. "What are you, and are you good to eat?"

I must still smell like the wolves, thought Ivan.

He stepped out from the hallway and into the vault. "I'm an Enigma, and I'm delicious."

The dragon swung toward the sound of his voice. As his great head came around, Ivan raised his bow and shot an arrow straight up into the dragon's eye.

The dragon screamed in pain and let out a long, fiery breath. He swung his head to and fro. Ivan aimed again, but the dragon was swinging his head too wildly: a second arrow would never hit its mark. Well, now he would find out if the Captain's charm worked. He ran across the floor of the vault, ignoring the dragon's flames, and picked up Sir Albert's sword. It was still warm, but had cooled down enough for him to raise it.

The pain had begun the moment the arrow entered the dragon's eye, but he tried not to pay attention. He did not want to think about how bad it would get. Where was the dragon's neck? It was still swinging wildly, but he brought the sword down just as it swung back toward him. The sword severed the dragon's neck cleanly in two, and his head rolled over the floor.

Ivan screamed from the pain and collapsed. He lay next to the dragon's head, with his eyes closed, unable to rise. Then, he felt something rough and wet on his cheek. He opened his eyes. Blanchefleur was licking him.

"Blanchefleur," he said weakly. "What are you doing here?"

"I followed you, of course," she said.

"But I never saw you."

"Of course not." She sat on the floor next to him as he slowly sat up. "Excellent shot, by the way. They'll call you Ivan Dragonslayer now, you know."

"Oh, I hope not," he said.

"It's inevitable."

The King met him with an embrace that made Ivan uncomfortable. "Welcome home, Ivan Dragonslayer! I shall have my attorney draw up the papers to make you my heir, and here of course is my lovely Alethea, who will become your bride. A royal wedding will attract tourists to the city, which will help with the rebuilding effort."

Princess Alethea crossed her arms and looked out the window. Even from the back, she seemed angry.

"Forgive me, Your Majesty," said Ivan, "but I have no wish to marry the Princess, and I don't think she wants to marry me either. We don't even know each other."

Princess Alethea turned and looked at him in astonishment. "Thank you!" she said. "You're the first person who's made any sense all day. I'm glad you slayed the dragon, but I don't see what that has to do with getting my hand in marriage. I'm not some sort of prize at a village fair."

"And I would not deprive you of a kingdom," said Ivan. "I have no wish to be king."

"Oh, goodness," said Alethea, "neither do I! Ruling is deadly dull. You can have the kingdom and do what you like with it. I'm going to university, to become an astronomer. I've wanted to be an astronomer since I was twelve."

"But . . ." said the King.

"Well then, it's decided, " said the Lady. "Ivan, you'll spend the rest of your apprenticeship here, in the palace, learning matters of state."

"But I want to go back to the wolves," said Ivan. He saw the look on the Lady's face: she was about to say no. He added, hurriedly, "If I can go back, just for the rest of my apprenticeship, I'll come back here and stay as long as you like, learning to be king. I promise."

"All right," said the Lady.

He nodded, gratefully. At least he would have spring in the mountains, with his pack.

I van and Blanchefleur rode north, not on a farm horse this time, but on a mare from the King's stables. As night fell, they stopped by a stream. The mountains were ahead of them, glowing in the evening light.

"You know, before we left, Tailcatcher asked me again," said Blanchefleur. "He thought that my time with you was done, that I would go back to the Castle in the Forest with my mother. I could have."

"Why didn't you?" asked Ivan.

"Why did you refuse the hand of the Princess Alethea? She was attractive enough."

"Because I didn't want to spend the rest of my life with her," said Ivan. "I want to spend it with you, Blanchefleur."

"Even though I'm a cat?"

"Even though."

She looked at him for a moment, then said, "I'm not always a cat, you know." Suddenly, sitting beside him was a girl with short white hair, wearing a white fur jacket and trousers. She had Blanche-fleur's eyes.

"Are you—are you Blanchefleur?" he asked. He stared at her. She was and she was not the white cat.

"Of course I am, idiot," she said. "I think you're going to make a good king. You'll have all the knowledge in the world to guide you, and any pain you cause, you'll have to feel yourself, so you'll be fair and kind. But you'll win all your battles. You'll hate it most of the time and wish you were back with the wolves or in Professor Owl's tower, or even taking care of the lizards. That's why you'll be good."

"And you'll stay with me?" he asked, tentatively reaching over and taking her hand.

"Of course," she said. "Who else is going to take care of you, Ivan?"

Together, they sat and watched the brightness fade from the mountain peaks and night fall over the Wolfwald. When Ivan lay down to sleep, he felt the white cat curl up next to his chest. He smiled into the darkness before slipping away into dreams.

Mr. Fox

When I first fell in love with Mr. Fox, he warned me:
You can't trust me, my dear.
Just when you think I am there,
I am gone, I am nowhere.
Look, I'm wearing a mask. Who does that? Thieves.
By the time the autumn leaves have fallen,
you will mourn my absence.

And yet, I couldn't help it. After all,
he was wearing such a dashing red coat,
like a soldier. He had such a twinkle in his eye.
He danced so nimbly, holding my hands
in paws on which he wore black kid gloves.
His tail ended in a white tuft.
I knew about the others, of course—or at least
I'd heard rumors. I knew he was no innocent.
I knew about the one who had drowned
herself in a river, her muslin gown floating
around her. I knew about the one who had locked
herself away in a convent.

How does one fall out of love with a thief
who has already stolen one's heart?
But I was cautious: I went to his castle in the woods.
Be bold, said the sign above the gate. *Be bold.*
But not too bold. I have never been good
at listening to advice, or taking it.
I was too bold, as usual.

What did I find? First, a pleasant parlor,
with blue silk curtains and rosewood furniture,

perfectly charming. Then, a library
filled with books, from Shakespeare to W. B. Yeats.
A kitchen, with no implements more dangerous
than a paring knife, beside a barrel of apples
waiting to be turned into cider.
Bathrooms with modern plumbing, a dining room
that contained a mahogany table, seldom used,
judging by the dust. But where was his secret chamber?
There must be one. On top of a desk in his study,
I'd seen a photograph of the girl who drowned,
beside a vase of lilies, like a memorial.

And there it was, at the end of a carpeted hallway.
I knew what it must lead to, that small door.
It was locked, of course, but I took out my lockpick tools
(if he was a thief, I was another).
It opened easily.

There was no blood on the floor. There were
no dead, dismembered wives hanging from hooks.
Instead, the walls were covered with masks:
fox, badger, mole, boar, weasel,
otter, squirrel, even one that resembled a tree.
All the masks he had worn, presumably.
And on one wall, opposite the window,
which badly needed washing, was a portrait
of an ordinary man with sandy hair
and tired eyes.

I locked the room behind me. At our wedding,
he said, "Are you sure, my dear?" with a toothy grin
that seemed wicked, but was, I thought, a little anxious.
"To marry the dangerous Mr. Fox?" I asked.
"Who knows, you might gobble me up,
but I'll take my chances." He seemed satisfied,
and swung me into a waltz. There's a moral to this story:
ladies, have your own set of lockpick tools. Also,
be bold and wise and cunning,
like a fox.

What Her Mother Said

Go, my child, through the forest
to your grandmother's house, in a glade
where poppies with red mouths grow.

In this basket is an egg laid
three days ago,
the three days our Lord lay sleeping,
unspotted, from a white hen.
In this basket is also a skein
of wool, without stain,
unspun. And a comb that the bees
industriously filled
from the clover in the far pasture,
unmown since the sun
thawed it, last spring.

If you can take it without breaking
anything, I will give you
this ring.

Stay, child, and I'll give you this cap
to wear, so the forest creatures whose eyes
blink from the undergrowth will be aware
that my love protects you. The creatures
lurking beneath the trees,
weasels and stoats and foxes, and worse
than these.

And child, you must be wise
in the forest.

When the wolf finds you, remember:
be courteous, but evasive. No answer
is better than a foolish one.

If you stray from the path, know
that I strayed also. It is no great matter,
so long as you mark the signs:
where moss grows on bark, where a robin
builds her nest. The sun
sailing west.

But do not stop to gather
the hawthorn flowers, nor yet
the red berries which so resemble
coral beads. They are poisonous.
And do not stop to listen
to the reeds.

He must not be there first,
at your grandmother's house.

When your grandmother serves you,
with a silver spoon, on a dish
like a porcelain moon, Wolf Soup,
remember to say your grace
before you eat.

And know that I am pleased
with you, my child.

But remember, when returning through the forest,
kept warm against the night by a cloak
of the wolf's pelt:
the hunter is also a wolf.

Snow, Blood, Fur

She looks at herself in the full-length mirror of the bridal salon. She resembles a winter landscape, hills and hollows covered with snow, white and sparkling. She is the essence of purity, as though all that has ever blown through her is a chill wind. The veil falls and falls to her feet. She shivers.

"Are you cold, Rosie?" her mother asks.

She shakes her head, but she is cold, or rather she is Cold, a Snow Queen. If she breathed on the mirror, it would frost.

"Well, you look beautiful. Just beautiful. Nana would have been so proud."

❧

When she gets home, she goes up to her bedroom and opens the closet door. In one corner, in a wooden toybox she has kept from her childhood, is the wolf skin. She puts it on, draping it around her shoulders, then steps into the closet, pulls the door closed behind her, and sits down beside a parade of high-heeled shoes.

It is dark, as dark as she imagines it must have been in the belly of the wolf.

❧

Sometimes she still has nightmares.

She is walking through the forest. Pine needles and oak leaves crunch under her boots. Once in a while, blackberry bushes pull at her dress so she has to stop and untangle the canes. She is wearing the red cloak her grandmother knit and felted. In it, she looks like a Swiss girl, demure, flaxen-haired: a Christmas angel. Her grandmother gave it to her for her sixteenth birthday.

Suddenly, on the path ahead of her is the wolf. Dark fur, slavering red mouth. Sharp, pricked ears, yellow eyes as wild as undiscovered countries. Or it is a young man, a hunter by his outfit. He has a tweed cap on his head with a feather in it, and is carrying a rifle. When he sees her, he bows, although she cannot tell if he is serious or mocking her.

"Aren't you afraid of the wolf, Mistress Rose? He has been seen in this forest. Perhaps I should escort you, wherever you might be going."

In her basket is a bottle of blackberry cordial, a small cake with currants. She is taking them to her grandmother, who has rheumatism. She has been told to beware wolves . . . and young men.

She shakes her head, eyes down. Hurriedly, she passes him, but as she is about to reach the bend in the path that will take her out of his sight, she turns back, just once, to look.

The wolf is standing in the middle of the path. Then, he disappears through the trees, off the path, where she is not allowed to go.

When she reaches her grandmother's house—small, tidy, with green shutters, apples ripening on the crooked tree, bees dancing around the skep—she knocks on the door. Hearing no answer, she opens it. There is no one in the parlor. She puts the cordial and cake in the pantry, leaves the basket on the kitchen table.

"Nana!" she calls. Could her grandmother be asleep?

In the bedroom, which smells of lavender, all she sees on the bed is the young man, naked. She has never seen a naked man before. He is beautiful, and grotesque, and frightening.

"Rosie Red, come to bed," he says. "You see, I have gotten here before you."

She takes off the red cloak.

༄

"Rosie!" her mother calls. "The florist is here with the centerpiece. Rosie, where are you?"

She knows what it will look like: lilies and gladiolas, so perfect they seem to be artificial. Scentless.

It is very quiet in the closet. It is very dark. She draws up her knees and puts her arms around them.

&

When she wakes up, the wolf is lying next to her. Where she lay, the sheets are spotted with blood. He has left his rifle on the chair, beside his discarded clothing.

She rises, still naked. Her father taught her how to use a rifle. One shot, and his body jumps on the bed. He yelps, although she does not know if he has woken up or passed directly from dreams into death. Two shots, and he lies still.

&

Her fiancé works for an accounting firm.

"Leroy has such a good job," says her mother. "He'll take care of you, Rosie. What more could any woman want?"

When he touches her, she shudders, as though his fingers were made of ice.

&

The police say she is very brave. Did they not find the remains of her grandmother at the edge of the woods, buried under oak leaves? Mauled—that is the only word. Mauled, gnawed, half-eaten.

They make her sit and drink a glass of blackberry cordial—for the shock, they say.

There is blood on the bed, a great deal of blood. It is the wolf's blood, they say, and she nods.

Later, her mother will bleach the sheets, but whenever she looks at them, she will think there was blood here, and here, and here.

&

"Rosie, the cake has arrived!" It has tiers and tiers of vanilla sponge iced with fondant, topped with sugar roses.

She imagines the table downstairs, in the dining room. The cake, the flowers, the gifts on display: Limoges dessert plates, engraved demitasse spoons.

&

Wearing the wolf skin, she does not have to be herself anymore. She does not have to be Rose. She can be something else entirely: pain, longing, anger. She can be silence if she wants to. She can be the word "no."

ℰℛ

And what about Leroy? He is no wolf.

But wolves, she has learned, are not the dangerous ones after all.

ℰℛ

This is a fairy tale, so all times are the same time: all times are now. She is always walking down the path, letting the white silk slip fall to her feet, pointing the rifle at the sleeping wolf, telling the story—the only story that makes sense—to the policeman. She is always trying on her wedding dress. It is always the season for blackberries and small red apples. She is always sitting in the darkness, warm and safe. She is always running through the forest, under oaks and pines.

ℰℛ

All she wants is the wolf's pelt, made into a cloak. Her mother does not think it is suitable, but her father consults the furrier. The red cloak has grown too small for her; she will wear the fur cloak, so much warmer in winter.

She wears it to visit her grandmother's grave, in the parish churchyard. "Nana," she says to the headstone. "Nana, I'm so sorry."

ℰℛ

She is fairly certain that if she wears the white dress, the one that makes her look immaculate, the one she may someday be buried in, drops of blood will appear on the bodice. Then streaks will run down the skirt. It will turn as red as a poppy among the wheat, as a flame on a match.

She rises, opens the closet door, and climbs out the window into the branches of the oak tree, then drops down on all fours and lopes, slowly, knowing that no one is watching, toward the forest.

She only stops once, to howl.

The Red Shoes

There are days
when I too want to cut off my feet.

Days on which I desire too much, on which I am filled
with longing for what I don't have, and may never.
When I feel that black hole in my chest
(like a manhole missing its cover)
into which things fall: my phone, the alarm clock,
the bulletin board on the wall,
the to-do list on my desk,
all my best intentions, and I think,
who needs feet? Especially
feet in red shoes.

Once you put the red shoes on,
you can never take them off.
I put them on when I was fifteen
and first fell in love,
and first wanted to live
anywhere but where I was living.

I thought, *Let me be wild. Let me dance, just a little.*
The red shoes never take you anywhere sensible.
They will take you to Paris
when your credit card is maxed out.

That, of course, is when I first wanted to become
a writer. One of the incorrigible.

But sometimes you get tired
of dancing everywhere: down the street,
on the subway.

And you think, I could just take a hatchet to them.
Karen did it, and she's up in heaven
somewhere, where good girls go.
She no longer wants anything.
She stopped writing long ago.

But what about Hans? Because he had a pair as well.
I suspect he's tap-dancing
in the hell writers make for themselves,
red shoes flashing (his had spangles).
He could never give up desire,
no matter how hard he tried.
He was ugly, and therefore wanted everything.
(As we are all ugly, if not outside, then inside,
all ducklings who only occasionally
recognize our swan parentage.)
He tried very hard to be good,
but kept falling in love,
which is a disadvantage.

So here I am, red shoes on (they never come off):
sometimes they are sandals, sometimes rain boots.
And I don't know what to do with them except keep walking,
which is also dancing, because although I may tire,
they don't.

Girl, Wolf, Woods

There are days on which I am the girl in the woods
in my red cap, jaunty, with my basket, plentiful,
wearing my innocence like a placard.

There are days on which I am the wolf, slavering
for either seedcake or a grandmother,
on which I am a hunger waiting
to be fed, a need, a desire.

There are days on which I am the woods,
silent, impenetrable.

Let me wander from the path, gathering flowers,
for night comes all too soon.

Feed me, for I am starved.
I want wine and cakes and meat. I want
the girl in the red cap and neat
apron. I want to crunch her bones.
I want to lope through darkness.

Let me be still, let me grow and feel
sunlight on my arms, which are also branches.
Let me hear birdsong.

There was a girl with a red cap,
a *chaperon* as they called it in that region,
which was famed for lace-making.
She ventured into the woods. The sun
was shining, but it was cool under the trees.

There, she met a wolf who was hungry
not for herself, but for her pups,
born late in the season, whom she was nursing.
Give me wine, she said, so I may be strong,
give me seedcake, or I will gobble up
your grandmother, and then you.

The girl knelt and said, here is wine,
here is cake, here is meat, a cold chicken leg
wrapped in a napkin, packed in the basket
by my mother, who embroidered this apron
with a row of red hearts.
I was taking it to my grandmother,
who has rheumatism and cannot run far,
but would be tough anyway.
Come, eat. I will share it with you.

The branches above sighed
as the wind passed through them,
and farther down the path, in a cottage
surrounded by lavender and sage,
among which bees were gathering
nectar from the flowers,
her grandmother was snoring.

That is not how the story goes, you insist.
But that is how I prefer to tell it.

Red as Blood
and White as Bone

I am an orphan. I was born among these mountains, to a wood-cutter and his wife. My mother died in childbirth, and my infant sister died with her. My father felt that he could not keep me, so he sent me to the sisters of St. Margarete, who had a convent farther down the mountain on which we lived, the Karhegy. I was raised by the sisters on brown bread, water, and prayer.

This is a good way to start a fairy tale, is it not?

When I was twelve years old, I was sent to the household of Baron Orso Kalman, whose son was later executed for treason, to train as a servant. I started in the kitchen, scrubbing the pots and pans with a brush, scrubbing the floor on my hands and knees with an even bigger brush. Greta, the German cook, was bad-tempered, as was the first kitchen maid, Agneta. She had come from Karberg, the big city at the bottom of the Karhegy—at least it seemed big, to such a country bumpkin as I was then. I was the second kitchen maid and slept in a small room that was probably a pantry, with a small window high up, on a mattress filled with straw. I bathed twice a week, after Agneta in her bathwater, which had already grown cold. In addition to the plain food we received as servants, I was given the leftovers from the baron's table after Greta and Agneta had picked over them. That is how I first tasted chocolate cake, and sausages, and beer. And I was given two dresses of my very own. Does this not seem like much? It was more than I had received at the convent. I thought I was a lucky girl!

I had been taught to read by the nuns, and my favorite thing to read was a book of fairy tales. Of course the nuns had not given me such a thing. A young man who had once stayed in the convent's guesthouse had given it to me, as a gift. I was ten years old, then. One of my duties was herding the goats. The nuns were famous for a goat's milk cheese, and so many of our chores had to do with the goats, their care and feeding. Several times, I met this man up in the mountain pastures. (I say *man*, but he must have been quite young still, just out of university. To me he seemed dreadfully old.) I was with the goats, he was striding on long legs, with a walking stick in his hand and a straw hat on his head. He always stopped and talked to me, very politely, as he might talk to a young lady of quality.

One day, he said, "You remind me of a princess in disguise, Klara, here among your goats." When I told him that I did not know what he meant, he looked at me in astonishment. "Have you never read any fairy tales?" Of course not. I had read only the Bible and my primer. Before he left the convent, he gave me a book of fairy tales, small but beautifully illustrated. "This is small enough to hide under your mattress," he said. "Do not let the nuns see it, or they will take it from you, thinking it will corrupt you. But it will not. Fairy tales are another kind of Bible, for those who know how to read them."

Years later, I saw his name again in a bookstore window and realized he had become a poet, a famous one. But by then he was dead. He had died in the war, like so many of our young men.

I followed his instructions, hiding the book under my mattress and taking it out only when there was no one to see me. That was difficult at the convent, where I slept in a room with three other girls. It was easier in the baron's house, where I slept alone in a room no one else wanted, not even to store turnips. And the book did indeed become a Bible to me, a surer guide than that other Bible written by God himself, as the nuns had taught. For I knew nothing of Israelites or the building of pyramids or the parting of seas. But I knew about girls who scrubbed floors and grew sooty sleeping near the hearth, and fish who gave you wishes (although I had never been given one), and was not Greta, our cook, an ogress? I'm sure she was. I regarded fairy tales as infallible guides to life, so I did not complain at the hard work I was given, because perhaps someday I would meet an old woman in the forest, and she would tell me that I was a princess in disguise. Perhaps.

The day on which *she* came was a cold, dark day. It had been raining for a week. Water poured down from the sky, as though to drown us all, and it simply did not stop. I was in the kitchen, peeling potatoes. Greta and Agneta were meeting with the housekeeper, Frau Hoffman, about a ball that was to take place in three days' time. It would celebrate the engagement of the baron's son, Vadek, to the daughter of a famous general, who had fought for the Austro-Hungarian emperor in the last war. Prince Radomir himself was staying at the castle. He had been hunting with Vadek Kalman in the forest that covered the Karhegy until what Greta called this unholy rain began. They had been at school together, Agneta told me. I found it hard to believe that a prince would go to school, for they never did in my tales. What need had a prince for schooling, when his purpose in life was to rescue fair maidens from the dragons that guarded them, and fight ogres, and ride on carpets that flew through the air like aeroplanes? I had never in my life seen either a flying carpet or an aeroplane: to me, they were equally mythical modes of transportation.

I had caught a glimpse of the general's daughter when she first arrived the day before, with her father and lady's maid. She was golden-haired, and looked like a porcelain doll under her hat, which Agneta later told me was from Paris. The lady's maid had told Frau Hoffman, who had told Greta, and the news had filtered down even to me. But I thought a Paris hat looked much like any other hat, and I had no interest in a general's daughter. She did not have glass slippers, and I was quite certain she could not spin straw into gold. So what good was she?

I was sitting, as I have said, in the kitchen beside the great stone hearth, peeling potatoes by a fire I was supposed to keep burning so it could later be used for roasting meat. The kitchen was dark, because of the storm outside. I could hear the steady beating of rain on the windows, the crackling of wood in the fire. Suddenly, I heard a *thump, thump, thump* against the door that led out to the kitchen garden. What could it be? For a moment, my mind conjured images out of my book: a witch with a poisoned apple, or Death himself. But then I realized it must be Josef, the under-gardener. He often knocked on that door when he brought peas or asparagus from the garden and made cow-eyes at Agneta.

"A moment," I cried, putting aside the potatoes I had been peeling, leaving the knife in a potato near the top of the basket so I could find it again easily. Then I went to the door.

When I pulled it open, something that had been leaning against it fell inside. At first I could not tell what it was, but it moaned and turned, and I saw that it was a woman in a long black cloak. She lay crumpled on the kitchen floor. Beneath her cloak she was naked: her white legs gleamed in the firelight. Fallen on the ground beside her was a bundle, and I thought: *Beggar woman. She must be sick from hunger.*

Greta, despite her harshness toward me, was often compassionate to the beggar women who came to our door—war widows, most of them. She would give them a hunk of bread or a bowl of soup, perhaps even a scrap of meat. But Greta was not here. I had no authority to feed myself, much less a woman who had wandered here in the cold and wet.

Yet there she lay, and I had to do something.

I leaned down and shook her by the shoulders. She fell back so that her head rolled around, and I could see her face for the first time. That was no cloak she wore, but her own black hair, covering her down to her knees, leaving her white arms exposed. And her white face . . . well. This was a different situation entirely. It was, after all, within my area of expertise, for although I knew nothing at all about war widows, I knew a great deal about lost princesses, and here at last was one. At last something extraordinary was happening in my life. I had waited a long time for this—an acknowledgment that I was part of the story. Not one of the main characters of course, but perhaps one of the supporting characters: the squire who holds the prince's horse, the maid who brushes the princess's hair a hundred times each night. And now story had landed with a thump on the kitchen floor.

But what does one do with a lost princess when she is lying on the kitchen floor? I could not lift her—I was still a child, and she was a grown woman, although not a large one. She had a delicacy that I thought appropriate to princesses. I could not throw water on her—she was already soaking wet. And any moment Greta or Agneta would return to take charge of my princess, for so I already thought of her. Finally, I resorted to slapping her cheeks until she opened her eyes—they were as deep and dark as forest pools.

"Come with me, Your Highness," I said. "I'll help you hide." She stood, stumbling a few times so that I thought she might fall. But she followed me to the only place I knew to hide her—my own small room.

"Where is . . ." she said. They were the first words she had said to me. She looked around as though searching: frightened, apprehensive. I went back to the kitchen and fetched her bundle, which was also soaked. When I handed it to her, she clutched it to her chest.

"I know what you are," I said.

"What . . . I am? And what is that?" Her voice was low, with an accent. She was not German, like Frau Hoffman, nor French, like Madame Francine, who did the baroness's hair. It was not any accent I had heard in my short life.

"You are a princess in disguise," I said. Her delicate pale face, her large, dark eyes, her graceful movements proclaimed who she was, despite her nakedness. I, who had read the tales, could see the signs. "Have you come for the ball?" *What country did you come from?* I wanted to ask. *Where does your father rule?* But perhaps that would have been rude. Perhaps one did not ask such questions of a princess.

"Yes . . . Yes, of course," she said. "What else would I have come for?"

I gave her my nightgown. It came only to her shins, but otherwise fitted her well enough, she was so slender. I brought her supper—my own supper, it was, but I was too excited to be hungry. She ate chicken off the bone, daintily, as I imagined a princess would. She did not eat the potatoes or cabbage—I supposed they were too common for her. So I finished them myself.

I could hear Greta and Agneta in the kitchen, so I went out to finish peeling the potatoes. Agneta scolded me for allowing the fire to get low. There was still meat to roast for the baron's supper, while Greta made a cream soup and Agneta dressed the cucumber salad. Then there were pots and pans to clean, and the black range to scrub. All the while, I smiled to myself, for I had a princess in my room.

I finished sweeping the ancient stone floor, which dated back to Roman times, while Greta went on about what we would need to prepare for the ball, how many village women she would hire to help with the cooking and baking for that night. And I smiled because I had a secret: my princess was going to the ball, and neither Greta nor Agneta would know.

When I returned to my room, the princess was fast asleep on my bed, under my old wool blanket that was ragged at the edges. I prepared to sleep on the floor, but she opened her eyes and said, "Come, little one," holding the blanket open for me. I crawled in and lay next to her. She was warm, and she curled up around me with her chin against my shoulder. It was the warmest and most comfortable I had ever been. I slept soundly that night.

The next day, I woke to find that she was already up and wearing my other dress.

"Today, you must show me around the castle, Klara," she said. Had she heard Greta or Agneta using my name the night before? The door was not particularly thick. She had not told me her name, and I did not have the temerity to ask for it.

"But if we are caught," I said, "we will be in a great deal of trouble!"

"Then we must not be caught," she said, and smiled. It was a kind smile, but there was also something shy and wild in it that I did not understand. As though the moon had smiled, or a flower.

"All right," I said. I opened the door of my room carefully. It was dawn, and light was just beginning to fall over the stones of the kitchen, the floor and great hearth. Miraculously, the rain had stopped overnight. Greta and Agneta were—where? Greta was probably still snoring in her nightcap, for she did not rise until an hour after me, to prepare breakfast. And Agneta, who also rose at dawn, was probably out fetching eggs and vegetables from Josef. She liked to take her time and smoke a cigarette in the garden. None of the female servants were allowed to smoke in the castle. I had morning chores to do, for there were more potatoes to peel for breakfast, and as soon as Agneta returned, I would need to help her make the mayonnaise.

But when would I find such a good opportunity? The baron and his guests would not be rising for hours, and most of the house servants were not yet awake. Only the lowest of us, the kitchen maids and bootblacks, were required to be up at dawn.

"This way," I said to my princess, and I led her out of the kitchen, into the hallways of the castle, like a great labyrinth. Frightened that I might be caught, and yet thrilled at the risk we were taking, I showed her the front hall, with the Kalman coat of arms hanging from the ceiling, and then the reception room, where paintings of the Kalmans and their horses stared down at us with disapproval. The horses were as disapproving as their masters. I opened the doors to the library, to me the most magical room in the house—two floors of books I would never be allowed to read, with a spiral staircase going up to a balcony that ran around the second floor. We looked out the windows at the garden arranged in parterres, with regular paths and precisely clipped hedges, in the French style.

"Is it not very grand?" I asked.

"Not as grand as my house," she replied. And then I remembered that she was a princess and likely had her own castle, much grander than a baron's.

Finally, I showed her the ballroom, with its ceiling painted like the sky and heathen gods and goddesses in various states of undress looking down at the dancers below.

"This is where you will dance with Prince Radomir," I said.

"Indeed," she replied. "I have seen enough, Klara. Let us return to the kitchen before you get into trouble."

As we scurried back toward the kitchen, down a long hallway, we heard voices coming from one of the rooms. As soon as she heard them, the princess put out her hand so I would stop. Softly, she stepped closer to the door, which was partly open.

Through the opening, I could see what looked like a comfortable parlor. There was a low fire in the hearth, and a man was sprawled on the sofa, with his feet up. I moved a few inches so I could see his face—it was Vadek Kalman.

"We'll miss you in Karelstad," said another man, sitting beyond where I could see him. "I suppose you won't be returning after the wedding?"

Had they gotten up so early? But no, the baron's son was still in evening dress. They had stayed up all night. Drinking, by the smell. Drinking quite a lot.

"And why should I not?" asked Vadek. "I'm going to be married, not into a monastery. I intend to maintain a social life. Can you imagine staying here, in this godforsaken place, while the rest of you are living it up without me? I would die of boredom, Radomir." So he was talking to the prince. I shifted a little, trying to see the prince, for I had not yet managed to catch a glimpse of him. After all, I was only a kitchen maid. What did he look like?

"And if your wife objects? You don't know yet—she might have a temper."

"I don't know a damn thing about her. She hasn't said two words to me since she arrived. She's like a frightened mouse, doing whatever her father the general tells her. Just the same as in Vienna. I tell you, the whole thing was put together by her father and mine. It's supposed to be a grand alliance. Grandalliance. A damn ridiculous word . . ."

I heard the sound of glass breaking, the words "God damn it all," and then laughter. The princess stood perfectly still beside me. She was barely breathing.

"So he thinks there's going to be another war?"

"Well, don't you? It's going to be Germany this time, and Father wants to make sure we have contacts on the right side. The winning side."

"The Reich side, eh?" said the prince. I heard laughter again, and did not understand what was so funny. "I wish my father understood that. He doesn't want to do business with the Germans. Karel agrees with him—you know what a sanctimonious ass my brother can be. You have to, I told him. Or they'll do business with you. And to you."

"Well, if you're going to talk politics, I'm going to bed," said Vadek. "I get enough of it from my father. Looks like the rain's finally stopped. Shall we go for a walk through the woods later today? That other wolf is still out there."

"Are you sure you saw it?"

"Of course I'm sure. It was under the trees, in the shadows. I could swear it was watching you. Anyway, the mayor said two wolves had been spotted in the forest, a hunting pair. They're keeping the children in at night in case it comes close to the village. You know what he said to me when I told him you had shot one of them? *It's bad luck to kill the black wolves of the Karhegy*, he said. I told him he should be grateful, that you had probably saved the life of some miserable village brat. But he just shook his head. Superstitious peasant."

"Next time, remind him that he could be put in prison for criticizing the crown prince. Things will be different in this country when I am king, Vadek. That I can tell you."

Klara heard appreciative laughter.

"And what will you do with the pelt? It's a particularly fine one— the tanner said as much, when he delivered it."

"It will go on the floor of my study, on one side of my desk. Now I need another, for the other side. Yes, let's go after the other wolf—if it exists, as you say."

The princess pulled me away.

I did not like this prince, who joked about killing the black wolves. I was a child of the Karhegy, and had grown up on stories of the wolves, as black as night, that lived nowhere else in Europe. The nuns had told me they belonged to the Devil, who would come after any man that harmed them. But my friend the poet had told me they were an ancient breed, and had lived on the mountain long before the Romans had come or Morek had driven them out, leading his tribesmen on their small, fierce ponies and claiming Sylvania for his own.

Why would my princess want to marry him? But that was the logic of fairy tales: the princess married the prince. Perhaps I should not question it, any more than I would question the will of God.

She led me back down the halls—evidently, she had learned the way better than I knew it myself. I followed her into the kitchen, hoping Greta would still be asleep—but no, there she stood, having gotten up early to prepare a particularly fine breakfast for the future baroness. She was holding a rolling pin in her hand.

"Where in the world have you been, Klara?" she said, frowning. "And who gave you permission to wander away? Look, the potatoes are not yet peeled. I need them to make pancakes, and they still need to be boiled and mashed. Who the devil is this with you?"

I looked over at my princess, frightened and uncertain what to say. But as neatly as you please, she curtseyed and said, "I've come from the village, ma'am. Father Ilvan told me you need help in the kitchen, to prepare for the ball."

Greta looked at her skeptically. I could tell what she was thinking—this small woman with her long, dark hair and accented voice. Was she a Slav? A gypsy? The village priest was known equally for his piety and propensity to trust the most inappropriate people. He was generous to peddlers and thieves alike.

But she nodded and said, "All right, then. Four hands are faster than two. Get those potatoes peeled."

That morning we peeled and boiled and mashed, and whisked eggs until our arms were sore, and blanched almonds. While Greta was busy with Frau Hoffman and Agneta was gossiping with Josef, I asked my princess about her country. Where had she come from? What was it like? She said it was not far, and as beautiful as Sylvania, and yes, they spoke a different language there.

"It is difficult for me to speak your language, little one," she said. We were pounding the almonds for marzipan.

"Do you tell stories there?" I asked her.

"Of course," she said. "Stories are everywhere, and everyone tells them. But our stories may be different from yours. About the Old

Woman of the Forest, who grants your heart's desire if you ask her right, and the Fair Ladies who live in trees, and the White Stag, who can lead you astray or lead you home . . ."

I wanted to hear these stories, but then Agneta came in, and we could not talk again about the things that interested me without her or Greta overhearing. By the time our work was done, long after supper, I was so tired that I simply fell into bed with my clothes on. Trying to stay awake although my eyes kept trying to close, I watched my princess draw the bundle she had brought with her out from the corner where I had put it. She untied it, and down came spilling a long black . . . was it a dress? Yes, a dress as black as night, floor-length, obviously a ball gown. It had been tied with its own sleeves. Something that glittered and sparkled fell out of it, onto the floor. I sat up, awake now, wanting to see more clearly.

She turned and showed me what had fallen—a necklace of red beads, each faceted and reflecting the light from the single bare bulb in my room.

"Do you like it?" she asked.

"They are . . . what are they?" I had never seen such jewels, although I had read about fabulous gems in my fairy tale book. The beads were each the size of a hummingbird's egg, and as red as blood. Each looked as though it had a star at its center. She laid the dress on my bed—I reached over and felt it, surreptitiously. It was the softest velvet imaginable. Then she clasped the necklace around her neck. It looked incongruous against the patched dress she was wearing—my second best one.

"Wait, where is . . ." She looked at the floor where the necklace had fallen, then got down on her knees and looked under the bed, then searched again frantically in the folds of the dress. "Ah, there! It was caught in a buttonhole." She held up a large comb, the kind women used to put their hair up in the last century.

"Will you dress my hair, Klara?" she asked. I nodded. While she sat on the edge of my bed, I put her hair up, a little clumsily but the way I had seen the baroness dress her hair, which was also long, not bobbed or shingled. Finally, I put in the comb—it was as white as bone, indeed probably made of bone, ornately carved and with long teeth to catch the hair securely.

"There," I said. "Would you like to look in a mirror?" I held up a discarded shaving glass I had found one morning on the trash heap at the bottom of the garden. I used it sometimes to search my face for any signs of beauty, but I had found none yet. I was always disappointed to find myself an ordinary girl.

She looked at herself from one side, then the other. "Such a strange face," she said. "I cannot get used to it."

"You're very beautiful," I said. And she was, despite the patched dress. Princesses are, even in disguise. That's how you know.

"Thank you, little one. I hope I am beautiful enough," she said, and smiled.

That night, she once again slept curled around me, with her chin on my shoulder. I dreamed that I was wandering through the forest, in the darkness under the trees. I crossed a stream over mossy stones, felt the ferns brushing against my shins and wetting my socks with dew. I found the little red mushrooms that are poisonous to eat, saw the shy, wild deer of the Karhegy, with their spotted fawns. When I woke, my princess was already up and dressed.

"Potatoes," she said. "Your life is an endless field of potatoes, Klara." I nodded and laughed, because it was true.

That day, we helped prepare for the ball. We were joined by Marta, the daughter of the village baker, and Anna, the groom's wife, who had been taking odd jobs since her husband was kicked by one of the baron's horses. He was bedridden until his leg was fully healed, and on half-salary. We candied orange and lemon peels, and pulled pastry until it was as thin as a bedsheet, then folded it so that it lay in leaves, like a book. We soaked cherries in rum, and glazed almonds and walnuts with honey. I licked some off my fingers. Marta showed us how to boil fondant, and even I was permitted to pipe a single icing rose.

All the while, we washed dishes and swept the floor, which quickly became covered with flour. My princess never complained, not once, even though she was obviously not used to such work. She was clumsier at it than I was, and if we had not needed the help, I think Greta would have dismissed her. As it was, she looked at her several times, suspiciously. How could any woman not know how to pull pastry? Unless she was a gypsy and spent her life telling fortunes, traveling in a caravan . . .

There was no time to talk that day, so I could not ask how she would get to the ball. And that night, I fell asleep as soon as my head touched the pillow.

The next day, the day of the ball, we were joined by the two upstairs maids: Katrina, who was from Karberg like Agneta, and her cousin, whose name I have forgotten. They were most superior young women, and would not have set foot in the kitchen except for such a grand occasion. What a bustle there was that day in the normally quiet kitchen! Greta barking orders and Agneta barking them after her, and the chatter of women working, although my princess did not chatter of course, but did her work in silence. We made everything that could not have been made ahead of time, whisking the béchamel, poaching fish, and roasting the pig that would preside in state over the supper room, with a clove-studded orange in its mouth. We sieved broth until it was perfectly clear, molded liver dumplings into various shapes, and blanched asparagus.

Nightfall found us prepared but exhausted. Greta, who had been meeting one last time with Frau Hoffman, scurried in to tell us that the motorcars had started to arrive. I caught a glimpse of them when I went out to ask Josef for some sprigs of mint. Such motorcars! Large and black and growling like dragons as they circled around the stone courtyard, dropping off guests. The men in black tails or military uniforms, the women in evening gowns, glittering, iridescent. How would my princess look among them, in her simple black dress?

At last all the food on the long kitchen table—the aspics and clear soup, the whole trout poached with lemons, the asparagus with its accompanying hollandaise—was borne up to the supper room by footmen. It took two of them to carry the suckling pig. Later would go the cakes and pastries, the chocolates and candied fruit.

"Klara, I need your help," the princess whispered to me. No one was paying attention—Katrina and her cousin had already gone upstairs to help the female guests with their wraps. Marta, Anna, and Agneta were laughing and gossiping among themselves. Greta was off doing something important with Frau Hoffman. "I need to wash and dress," she said. And indeed, she had a smear of buttery flour across one cheek. She looked as much like a kitchen maid as a princess can look, when she has a pale, serious face and eyes as deep as forest pools, and long black hair that kept escaping the braid into which she had put it.

"Of course," I said. "There is a bathroom down the hall, beyond the water closet. No one will be using it tonight."

No one noticed as we slipped out of the kitchen. My princess fetched her dress, and then I showed her the way to the ancient bathroom shared by the female servants, with its metal tub.

"I have no way of heating the water," I said. "Usually Agneta boils a kettle, and I take my bath after her."

"That's all right," she said, smiling. "I have never taken a bath in hot water all my life."

What a strict regimen princesses followed! Never to have taken a bath in hot water . . . not that I had either, strictly speaking. But after Agneta had finished with it, the bathwater was usually still lukewarm.

I gave her one of the thin towels kept in the cupboard, then sat on a stool with my back to the tub, to give her as much privacy as I could while she splashed and bathed.

"I'm finished," she said finally. "How do I look, little one?"

I turned around. She was wearing the black dress, as black as night, out of which her shoulders and neck rose as though she were the moon emerging from a cloud. Her black hair hung down to her waist.

"I'll put it up for you," I said. She sat on the stool, and I recreated the intricate arrangement of the other night, with the white comb to hold it together. She clasped the necklace of red beads around her neck and stood.

There was my princess, as I had always imagined her: as graceful and elegant as a black swan. Suddenly, tears came to my eyes.

"Why are you crying, Klara?" she asked, brushing a tear from my cheek with her thumb.

"Because it's all true," I said.

She kissed me on the forehead, solemnly as though performing a ritual. Then she smiled and said, "Come, let us go to the ballroom."

"I can't go," I said. "I'm just the second kitchen maid, remember? You go . . . you're supposed to go."

She smiled, touched my cheek again, and nodded. I watched as she walked away from me, down the long hallway that led to other parts of the castle, the parts I was not supposed to enter. The white comb gleamed against her black hair.

And then there was washing-up to do.

It was not until several hours later that I could go to my room, lie on my bed exhausted, and think about my princess, dancing with Prince Radomir. I wished I could see her . . . and then I thought, *Wait, what about the gallery?* From the upstairs gallery one could look down through a series of five roundels into the ballroom. I could get up to the second floor using the back stairs. But then I would have to walk along several hallways, where I might meet guests of the baron. I might be caught. I might be sent back to the nuns—in disgrace.

But I wanted to see her dancing with the prince. To see the culmination of the fairy tale in which I had participated.

Before I could take too long to think about it, I sneaked through the kitchen and along the back hallway, to the staircase. Luckily, the second-floor hallways were empty. All the guests seemed to be down below—as I scurried along the gallery, keeping to the walls, I could hear the music and their chatter floating upward. On one side of the gallery were portraits of the Kalmans not important enough to hang in the main rooms. They looked at me as though wondering what in the world I was doing there. Halfway down the other side were the roundels, circular windows through which light shone on the portraits. I looked through the first one. Yes, there she was—easy to pick out, a spot of black in the middle of the room, like the center of a Queen Anne's lace. She was dancing with a man in a military uniform. Was he . . . I would be able to see better from the second window. Yes, the prince, for all the other dancers were giving them space. My princess was dancing with the prince—a waltz, judging by the music. Even I recognized that three-four time. They were turning round and round, with her hand on his shoulder and her red necklace flashing in the light of the chandeliers.

Were those footsteps I heard? I looked down the hall, but they passed—they were headed elsewhere. I put my hand to my heart, which was beating too fast, and took a long breath in relief. I looked back through the window.

My princess and Prince Radomir were gone. The Queen Anne's lace had lost its center.

Perhaps they had gone into the supper room? I waited, but they did not return. And for the first time, I worried about my princess. How would her story end? Surely she would get her happily ever after. I wanted, so much, for the stories to be true.

I waited a little longer, but finally I trudged back along the gallery, tired and despondent. It must have been near midnight, and

I had been up since dawn. I was so tired that I must have taken a
wrong turn, because suddenly I did not know where I was. I kept
walking, knowing that if I just kept walking long enough through
the castle hallways, I would eventually end up somewhere familiar.
Then, I heard her voice. A door was open—the same door, I suddenly realized, where we had listened two days ago.

She was in that room—why? The door was open several inches. I
looked in, carefully. She stood next to the fireplace. Beside her, holding one of her hands, was the prince. She was turned toward him, the
red necklace muted in the dim light of a single lamp.

"Closer, and farther, than you can guess," she said, looking at
him, with her chin raised proudly.

"Budapest? Perhaps you come from Budapest. Or Prague? Do
you come from Prague? Tell me your name. If you tell me your name,
I'll wager you I can guess where you come from in three tries. If I do,
will I get a kiss?"

"And if you don't?"

"Then you'll get a kiss. That's fair, isn't it?"

He drew her to him, circling her waist with his arm. She put
her arm around his neck, so that they stood clasped together. He
still held one of her hands. It was a private moment, and I felt that I
should go—but I could not. In my short life, I had never been to a
play, but I felt as audience members feel, having come to a climactic
moment. I held my breath.

"My name is meaningless in your language," she said. He
laughed, then leaned down and kissed her on the lips. They stood
there by the fireplace, his lips on hers, and I thought, *Yes, this is how
a fairy tale should end.*

I sighed, although without making a noise that might disturb
them. Then with the arm that had been around his neck, she reached
back and took the intricately carved comb out of her hair, so that
it tumbled down like nightfall. With a swift motion, she thrust the
sharp teeth of the comb into the side of his neck.

The prince threw back his head and screamed, like an animal
in the forest. He stumbled back, limbs flailing. There was blood
down his uniform, almost black against the red of his jacket. I was
so startled that for a moment I did nothing, but then I screamed as
well, and those screams—his maddened with pain, mine with fear—
echoed down the halls.

In a moment, a footman came running. "Shut up, you," he said when he saw me. But as soon as he looked into the room, his face grew pale, and he began shouting. Soon there were more footmen, and the baron, and the general, and then Father Ilvan. Through it all, my princess stood perfectly still by the fireplace, with the bloody comb in her hand.

When they brought the prince out on a stretcher, I crouched by the wall, but no one was paying attention to me. His head was turned toward me, and I saw his eyes, pale blue. Father Ilvan had not yet closed them.

They led her out, one footman on each side, holding her by the upper arms. She was clutching something. It looked like part of her dress, just as black, but bulkier. She did not look at me, but she was close enough that I could see how calm she was. Like a forest pool— deep and mysterious.

Slowly, I walked back to the kitchen. In my room, I drew up my knees and hugged them, then put my chin on my knees. The images played in my head, over and over, like a broken reel at the cinema: him bending down to kiss her, her hand drawing the comb out of her hair, the sharp, quick thrust. I had no way of understanding them. I had no stories to explain what had happened.

At last I fell asleep, and dreamed those images over and over, all night long.

In the morning, there was breakfast to prepare. As I fried sausages and potatoes, I heard Greta tell Agneta what had happened. She had heard it from Frau Hoffman herself: A foreign spy had infiltrated the castle. At least, she was presumed to be a foreign spy, although no one knew where she came from. Was she Slovakian? Yugoslavian? Bulgarian? Why had she wanted the prince dead?

She would not speak, although she would be made to speak. The baron had already telephoned the Royal Palace, and guards had been dispatched to take her, and the body of the prince, to Karelstad. They would arrive sometime that afternoon. In the meantime, she was locked in the dungeon, which had not held prisoners for a hundred years.

After breakfast, the baron himself came down to question us. The servants had been shown a sketch of a small, pale woman with long black hair, made by Father Ilvan. Katrina had identified her as one of the village women who had helped in the kitchen, in preparation for the ball. Why had she been engaged?

Because Father Ilvan had sent her, said Greta. But Father Ilvan had no knowledge of such a woman. Greta and Agneta were told to pack their bags. What had they been thinking, allowing a strange woman to work in the castle, particularly when the crown prince was present? If they did not leave that day, they would be put in the dungeon as well. And no, they would not be given references. I was too frightened to speak, to tell the baron that I had been the one to let her in. No one paid attention to me—I was too lowly even to blame.

By that afternoon, Marta, the baker's daughter, was the new cook, and I was her kitchen maid. In two days, I had caused the death of the prince and gotten promoted.

"Klara," she said to me, "I have no idea how we are to feed so many people, just the two of us. And Frau Hoffman says the royal guards will be here by dinnertime! Can you imagine?"

Then it was now or never. In an hour or two, I would be too busy preparing dinner, and by nightfall my princess—my spy?—would be gone, taken back to the capital for trial. I was frightened of what I was about to do, but felt that I must do it. In my life, I have often remembered that moment of fear and courage, when I took off my apron and sneaked out the door into the kitchen garden. It was the first moment I chose courage over fear, and I have always made the same choice since.

The castle had, of course, been built in the days before electric lights. Even the dungeon had windows. Once, Josef had shown them to me, when I was picking raspberries for a charlotte russe. Holding back the raspberry canes, he had said, "There, you see, little mouse, is the deep dark dungeon of the castle!" Although as far as I could tell it was just a bare stone room, with metal staples in the walls for chains. From the outside, the windows were set low into the castle wall, but from the inside they were high up in the wall of the dungeon—high enough that a tall man could not reach them. And they were barred.

It was late afternoon. Josef and the gardener's boy who helped him were nowhere in sight. I crawled behind the raspberry canes, getting scratched in the process, and looked through one of the barred windows.

She was there, my princess. Sitting on the stone floor, her black dress pooled around her, black hair hanging down, still clutching something black in her arms. She was staring straight ahead of her, as though simply waiting.

"Princess!" I said, low in case anyone should hear. There must be guards? But I could not see them. The dungeon door was barred as well. There was no way out.

She looked around, then up. "Klara," she said, and smiled. It was a strange, sad smile. She rose and walked over to the window, then stood beneath it, looking up at me, her face pale and tired in the dim light. Then I could see what she had been clutching: a wolf pelt, with the four paws and eyeless head hanging down.

"Why?" I asked. And then, for the first time, I began to cry. Not for Prince Radomir, but for the story. Because it had not been true, because she had allowed me to believe a lie. Because when Greta said she was a foreign spy, suddenly I had seen life as uglier and more ordinary than I had imagined, and the realization had made me sick inside.

"Klara," she said, putting one hand on the wall, as far up as she could reach. It was still several feet below the window. "Little one, don't cry. Listen, I'm going to tell you a story. Once upon a time— that's how your stories start, isn't it? Quietly, so the guards won't hear. They are around the corner, having their dinners. I can smell the meat. Once upon a time, there were two wolves who lived on the Karhegy. They were black wolves, of the tribe that has lived on the mountain since time out of mind. The forest was their home, dark and peaceful and secure. There they lived, there they hoped to some-day raise their children. But one day, a prince came with his gun, and he shot one of the wolves, who was carried away by the prince's men for his fine pelt. The other wolf, who was his mate, swore that she would kill the prince."

I listened intently, drying my face with the hem of my skirt.

"So she went to the Old Woman of the Forest and said, 'Grand-mother, you make bargains that are hard but fair. I will give you anything for my revenge.' And the Old Woman said, 'You shall have it. But you must give me your beautiful black pelt, and your danger-ous white teeth, and the blood that runs in your body. For such a revenge, you must give up everything.' And the wolf agreed. All these things she gave the Old Woman, who fashioned out of them a dress as black as night, and a necklace as red as blood, and a comb as white as bone. The old woman gave them to the wolf and said, 'Now our bargain is complete.' The wolf took the bundle the Old Woman had given her and stumbled out of the forest, for it was difficult walking on only two legs. On a rainy night, she made her way to the castle where the prince was staying. And the rest of the story, you know."

I stared down at her, not knowing what to say. Should I believe it? Or her? Common sense told me that she was lying, that she was a foreign spy and I was a fool. But then, I have never had much common sense. And that, too, has stood me in good stead.

"Klara, put your hand through the bars," she said.

I hesitated, then did as I was told.

She put the pelt down on the floor beside her, carefully as though it were a child, then unclasped the necklace of red beads. "Catch!" she said, and threw it up to me. I caught it—and then I heard boots echoing down the corridor. "Go now!" she said. "They're coming for me." I drew back my hand with the necklace in it and crawled away from the window. The sun was setting. It was time for me to return to the kitchen and prepare dinner. No doubt Marta was already wondering where I was.

When I got back to the kitchen, I learned that the royal guards had arrived. But they were too late—using the metal staples on the walls, my princess had hanged herself by her long black hair.

When I was sixteen, I left the baron's household. By that time, I was as good a cook as Marta could teach me to be. I knew how to prepare the seven courses of a formal dinner, and I was particularly skilled in what Marta did best: pastry. I think my pâte à choux was as good as hers.

In a small suitcase, I packed my clothes, and my fairy tale book, and the necklace that my wolf-princess had given me, which I had kept under my mattress for many years.

Perhaps it was not wise, moving to Karelstad in the middle of the German occupation. But as I have said, I am deficient in common sense—the sense that keeps most people safe and out of trouble. I let bedraggled princesses in out of the rain. I pack my suitcase and move to the capital with only a fortnight's wages and a reference from the baroness. I join the Resistance.

Although I did not know it, the café where I worked was a meeting-place for the Resistance. One of the young men who would come to the café, to drink coffee and read the newspapers, was a member. He had long hair that he did not wash often enough, and eyes of a startling blue, like evening in the mountains. His name was Antal Odon, and he was a descendent of the nineteenth-century poet

Amadeo Odon. He would flirt with me, until we became friends. Then he did not flirt with me any longer, but spoke with me solemnly, about Sylvanian poetry and politics. He had been at the university until the Germans came. Then, it no longer seemed worthwhile becoming a literature professor, so he had left. What was he doing with himself now, I asked him?

It was he who first brought me to a meeting of the Resistance, in the cellar of the café where I worked. The owner, a motherly woman named Malina who had given me both a job and a room above the café, told us about Sylvanians who had been taken that week—both Jews and political prisoners. The next day, I went to a jeweler on Morek Stras, with my necklace as red as blood. How much for this? I asked him. Are these beads worth anything?

He looked at them through a small glass, then told me they would be worth more individually. Indeed, in these times, he did not know if he could find a purchaser for the entire necklace. He had never seen such fine rubies in his life.

One by one, he sold them off for me, often to the wives of German officers. Little did they know that they were funding the Resistance. I kept only one of the beads for myself, the smallest. I wear it now on a chain around my neck. So you can see, Grandmother, that my story is true.

As a member of the Resistance, I traveled to France and Belgium and Denmark. I carried messages sewn into my brassiere. No one suspects a young girl, if she wears high heels and red lipstick, and laughs with the German officers, and looks down modestly when they light her cigarette. Once, I even carried a message to a small town in the Swiss mountains, to a man who was introduced to me as Monsieur Reynard. He looked like his father, as far as one can tell from official portraits—one had hung in the nunnery schoolroom. I was told not to curtsey, simply to shake his hand as though he were an ordinary Sylvanian. I did not tell him, *I saw your older brother die. I hope that someday you will once again return to Sylvania, as its king.*

With my friend Antal, I smuggled political refugees out of the country. By then, we were more than friends . . . We hoped someday to be married, when the war was over. But he was caught and tortured. He never revealed names, so you see he died a hero. The man I loved died a hero.

When the war ended and the Russian occupation began, I did not know what to do with myself. I had imagined a life with Antal, and he was dead. But there were free classes at the university, for those who had been peasants, if you could pass the exams. I was no longer a peasant exactly, but I told the examiners that my father had been a woodcutter on the Karhegy, and I passed with high marks, so I was admitted. I threw myself into work and took my degree in three years—in Sylvanian literature, as Antal would have, if he had lived. I thought I would find work in the capital, but the Ministry of Education said that teachers were needed in Karberg and the surrounding area, so I was sent here, to a school in the village of Orsolavilag, high in the mountains. There I teach students whose parents work in the lumber industry, or at one of the hotels for Russian and Austrian tourists.

When I first returned, I tried to find my father. But I learned that he had died long ago. He had been cutting wood while drunk, and had struck his own leg with an axe. The wound had become infected, and so he had died. A simple, brutal story. So I have no one left in the world. All I have left is my work.

I teach literature and history to the children of Orsolavilag . . . or such literature and history as I am allowed. We do not teach fairy tales, which the Ministry of Education thinks are decadent. We teach stories of good Sylvanian boys and girls who learn to serve the state. In them, there are no frogs who turn into princes, no princesses going to balls in dresses like the sun, moon, and stars. No firebirds. There are no black wolves of the Karhegy, or Fair Ladies who live in trees, or White Stag that will, if you are lost, lead you home. There is no mention even of you, Grandmother. Can you imagine? No stories about the Old Woman of the Forest, from whom all the stories come.

Within a generation, those stories will be lost.

So I have come to you, whose bargains are hard but fair. Give me stories. Give me all the stories of Sylvania, so I can write them down, and so our underground press in Karberg, for which we could all be sent to a prison camp, can publish them. We will pass them from hand to hand, household to household. For this, Grandmother, I will give you what my princess gave so long ago: whatever you ask. I have little left, anyhow. My only possession of value is a single red bead on a chain, like a drop of blood.

I am a daughter of these mountains, and of the tales. Once, I wanted to be in the tales themselves. When I was young, I had my part in one—a small part, but important. When I grew older, I had my part in another kind of story. But now I want to become a teller of tales. So I will sit here, in your hut on goose legs, which sways a bit like a boat on the water. Tell me your stories, Grandmother. I am listening . . .

The Gold-Spinner

There was a little man, I told him.

I gave the little man my rosary,
I gave the little man my ring,
my mother's ring, which she had given me
as she lay dying. A thin circlet of gold
with a garnet, fit for a commoner.

As I was a commoner, I reminded him.
Nothing magical about me.

Very well, he said. You may go
back to your father's mill. I have no use
for a miller's daughter without magic in her fingers.
I'll keep the three roomfuls of gold.

I walked away from the palace, still barefoot,
still dressed in rags, looking behind me
surreptitiously, afraid he would change his mind.
Afraid he would realize he'd been tricked.
I mean, what kind of name
is Rumpelstiltskin?

But he would have kept me spinning
in a succession of rooms, forever.

I passed my father's mill without entering,
either to greet or berate. I wanted you to be queen,
he had told me, after I said how could you
betray me like this?

You deserve that, you deserve better
than your mother. What kind of life
did I give her?

No, I wasn't going back there.

By mid-afternoon I had left the town,
I had forded the river, I had come
to unfamiliar fields. I sat me down
by a hedge on which a few late roses bloomed
and from a thorn I plucked a tuft of wool
left by a passing sheep. I spun,
twisting it between my fingers
as my mother had taught me.
She, too, had the gift.

I coiled the resulting thread
of thin, soft gold
around my wrist. Somewhere along the road
it would buy me bread.

Until then, there were crabapples
and blackberries to share with the birds.
And the road ahead of me,
leading I knew not where, but somewhere different
than the road behind.

Rumpelstiltskin

The little man
tore himself in two.
What did the two halves do
after that?
Fairy folk don't die
from such simple operations.

And no, they didn't hop about,
each on a single leg.
Each half was a complete
facsimile of the original,
except that one was reversed:
a mirror image of the other.
One was left-handed, the other right.

The two halves stared at each other.
Brother, said one,
I shall go into the forest:
I'm done with humanity.
Let millers' daughters ever after
suffer the consequences of their own folly.
I shall live alone, with only the birds and squirrels,
the occasional deer, for company.
I shall live off mushrooms, acorns, ferns,
eggs fallen from the nest, rose hips
and blackberries in summer: the forest's bounty.
Dress myself in moss, breathe slowly,
become like the rocks.
I shall call myself Rumpel,
if you've no objection.

None at all, said the other half.
I, however, want to see the world,
live as you have never dared to.
Start as a thief, steal coins from the rich,
food from the poor. Visit whorehouses.
Build my fortune, gamble with it—
win, lose, end up in debtor's prison.
Drink dirty water, and a year later
fine Burgundy, when I have regained my fortune
and more. I shall have estates
in Germany, in France. My mills will spew black smoke
over the countryside, manufacturing
fabric for elegant ladies, so they can wear
the latest fashions, my great looms
clacking and whirring like mechanical spiders.
That is the way to spin gold, brother.
When I am richer than the king,
he will offer me his daughter.
By then, I shall be Lord Stiltskin.

The two halves parted, with every sign
of mutual respect. Neither
chastised the other.
There were no recriminations.

In each of us
there is a thief and a saint.
The trouble of it is,
we cannot part them.

Goldilocks and the Bear

They met when they were children.

She was a thief,
yellow-haired, small for her age,
only twelve years old, already hardened
by poverty, already a noted pickpocket,
stealing into the bears' house.

He was a rube, a rustic,
or so she said then. A mark
is what she called him—
to his face, no less.

He was the one who found her in his bedroom,
trying to climb out the window,
and hid her in his closet
while his father raged:
who had stolen the carved wooden box
filled with gold coins, the profits
of their honey business?

He would not let her keep the coins.
He was not that much of a rube.

But while his father was talking to the constable,
a comical fellow straight out of Shakespeare,
he returned the box, saying he had found it
by the kitchen door, where the thief must have dropped it
on his way out. They should look in the forest—
he could be a mile away by now.

That night, he told her the coast was clear
and let her out the window.
At the last moment, before she made her escape,
she kissed him on the cheek
and laughed. That's the way she was
back then, fearless.

He got on with his life,
finishing school, then going into the business,
learning how to care for the bees,
how to keep them healthy,
taking extension classes on bee diseases:
mites and spores that endanger bees directly,
hive beetles that infect their homes,
wax moths that feed on honeycombs,
damaging the larvae.
He learned what to plant in the fields,
how to prune the trees in the orchard:
to produce lavender honey, and clover,
and linden-flower.

He learned how to mold the wax sculptures
sold in the gift shop.
His mother was particularly good at those.

Meanwhile, she worked with a gang
of child thieves out of a Dickens novel:
ragged clothes, solidarity pacts,
the possibility of incarceration.
She ended up in jail once, was broken out,
continued to steal until she was fifteen
and their leader suggested prostitution.
It was, he said, an honorable profession,
as old as thieving. And she such a pretty girl,
with that yellow hair: she was sure to do well.
He would, of course, take a small percentage.
The suggestion was punctuated
by his fist on the table, and a grin
she did not like the look of.

That night she climbed up to the bear's window—
she had not forgotten the location—
and knocked on the pane.
"Help me," she said when he opened it.
"I need help, and you're the only one
who's helped me before."

He listened patiently, then angrily:
three years' worth of exploits
and exploitation. She showed him her wrist
where the gang leader had once broken it.
She was still small and pale from malnutrition.

They dyed her hair brown with walnuts.
He got her a job in the honey business,
first in the gift shop, then because she showed interest,
taking care of the bees.

She had never seen anything so fascinating:
like a city of soft, furry bodies
moving in a mass, then in individual flight,
seemingly wild, erratic, but purposeful.
She loved to watch them among the lavender,
the dusting of yellow pollen on their fur.
There was something purely joyful about them,
and they were always making, making—
thieves, like her, taking the nectar,
but making wax catacombs, the golden honey
more precious, she thought, than coins.

He showed her how to work among the bees,
wearing thick cotton and a hat veiled with muslin,
which he did not need, protected by his pelt.
Eventually, he asked her to dinner
with his parents.

His mother said she was charming.
His father had a serious talk
with him: you can't trust humans, he said.

They're not like bears. Think of that thief, long ago,
who tried to take our gold.
They don't even sleep in winter,
which is unnatural, unbearlike.
If you have to fall for someone, can't it be
another bear from a good family,
like ours?

The bear explained that love
doesn't work like that.

When he asked her to marry him
beneath the linden branches,
she said, aren't you afraid
I might still be that girl?
That I might become a thief again?
You are, and you might, he said.
But I'm not my father. I've always been willing
to take risks, like letting you go that day
or trying new honey flavors. Look how well
the rhubarb honey turned out.

I'm not rhubarb honey, she said, laughing.
Close enough, he said, and kissed her.

Goldilocks and the bear lived to a grand old age
together. Their children could turn
into bears at will. One married a princess,
one joined the circus,
one took over the honey business.
They have five grandchildren.
Her hair is silver now.

Look how well her thievery turned out.
She got the gold, she got the bear,
she got the fields of clover,
the flowering orchard, the house filled with sunlight
and sweetness, like a jar of honey. The life
of a happy woman.

Sleeping With Bears

I. The Invitation

Dr. and Mrs. Elwood Barlow
request the honor of your presence
at the marriage of their daughter Rosalie
to Mr. T. C. Ursus
on Saturday the thirteenth of June
at one o'clock
at the First Methodist Church

Reception to follow in the Church Hall

II. The Bride

They are wealthy, these bears. Their friends come to the wedding in fur coats.

Rosie is wearing Mom's dress, let out at the waist. When Mom married, she was Miss Buckingham County. She shows us the tape measure. "That's what I was, twenty-two inches around the waist: can you imagine?" My sister, after years of jazzercize and Jane Fonda, is considerably thicker. When, I wonder, were women's waists replaced by abdominals? When cheerleaders started competing for state championships, I guess. Rosie was a cheerleader. Her senior year, our squad was fourth in state. That year she wore the class ring of the student council president, who was also the captain of the football team. She was in the homecoming court. She was furious when Lisa Callahan was elected queen.

After she graduated from Sweet Briar and began working as a legal secretary, she met a lawyer who was making sixty thousand a year. They started talking about having children, buying a Mercedes.

So I don't understand why she decided to marry a bear.

III. The Groom

O f course he comes from old money. *Ursus Americanus* has been in Virginia since before John Smith founded the Jamestown Colony. The family has gone down in the social scale. It doesn't own as much land as it used to, and what it does own is in the mountains, no good for livestock, no good for tobacco. No good for anything but timber. But there sure is a lot of timber.

Anyway, that's how Southern families are. Look at the Carters or Randolphs. If you haven't degenerated, you're not really old. If you want to join the First Families of Richmond, you'd better be able to produce an insane uncle, an aunt who lives on whiskey, to prove you're qualified.

We don't come from that kind of family. Mom is the daughter of a Baptist preacher from Arvonia. There was no whiskey in her house. She didn't even see a movie until she was seventeen. Dad was a step up, the son of the town's doctor. Grandpa Barlow didn't believe in evolution. I don't think he ever got over learning, in medical school, that men don't have a missing rib. Mom and Dad met in third grade. They went to the sock hop and held hands in church while sharing a hymnal. You can see their pictures in the Arvonia High School yearbook. Dad lists his future career as astronaut, Mom as homemaker. They were voted Most Likely to Get Married. They look clean, as though they just stepped out of a television show from the 1950s.

So maybe that's it, maybe Rosie's still mad that we didn't belong to the Richmond Country Club, that Dad didn't send her to Saint Gertrude's, where the daughters of the First Families learn geometry and which fork to use with the fish. That he didn't think of giving her a debutante ball. Mom's friends would have looked at her and said, with raised eyebrows, "My, isn't Rosie the society lady?"

And when I see them, the bears sitting on the groom's side of the church, I have to admit that they are aristocratic, like the Bear Kings of Norway, who sat on thrones carved from ice and ruled the Arctic tundra. (Nevertheless, they look perfectly comfortable in the heat, even in their fur coats.)

IV. The Procession

"What do you call him in private?" I ask Rosie. I've never dared call him anything other than Mr. Ursus. When a man—or bear—is six feet tall and over two hundred pounds, he commands respect.

"Catcher," she says. "That's his middle name, or maybe part of his first name. Trout Catcher. That's what his family calls him."

"How much do you really know about bears?" I ask. "Like, do you know what to cook him for dinner?"

"For goodness' sake, Blanche," she says. "Put the brush down, you're tangling my hair. Some of his relatives eat garbage, all right? I'll figure it out as I go along."

I wonder. In the library, I found a book about bears. *Ursus Americanus* eats acorns, melons, honey (including the bees), and gut piles left by hunters. I don't know what Rosie's going to do with gut piles.

I help her with the veil, which comes down to her fingernails, manicured yesterday and painted bubble gum pink. I wonder if bears like bubble gum? I hold her train as she walks along the gravel path from the minister's house, where she's been applying a final coat of mascara, to the church. I'm careful not to let her skirt trail on the gravel.

Mom's and Dad's friends are standing, the women in dresses from Lord and Taylor, the men in linen suits. The bears are standing, black and brown and the toffee color called gold. "Black bear" is a misnomer, really. They look like a forest of tree trunks, without leaves.

The organist plays the wedding march. This is Rosie's choice. She has no originality. Which again makes me wonder: why is she marrying a bear?

V. The Ceremony

Or perhaps I should ask, why is he marrying her?

When she first brought him home, Mom hid in the bathroom. Dad had to tell her repeatedly that bears don't eat people. That they're really quite gentle, except when their cubs are threatened. That they're probably more afraid of you than you are of them.

Still, Mom sat at the edge of her chair, moving the roast beef around on her plate, not reassured to see Catcher eating only peas and carrots, mashed potatoes.

"What do you do, Mr. Ursus?" asked Dad.

He managed the family property. Conservation land, most of it, in trust for future generations. You could call him a sort of glorified forest ranger. He laughed, or perhaps growled, showing incisors of a startling whiteness.

"Your children will never need dental work," said Dad.

Rosie was mortified. They hadn't gotten to that stage yet. I don't think she'd even kissed him good night.

She'll kiss him now, certainly, and I wait to see how it will happen: whether she will be swallowed by that enormous and powerful jaw. But he kisses her on the cheek. I can see his whiskers tickling her ear. I suppose the devouring will begin later.

VI. The Photographs

Don't get me wrong, I don't think he's going to eat her. Bears don't eat people, remember?

But I know the facts of life. When Mom married at eighteen, Grandma told her, "Just close your eyes and pray for children." When I was fifteen, Mom taught me what happens between men and women. Though I have to admit, she never said anything about bears.

When our photographs are taken, I stand next to the best man—or bear, Catcher's younger brother. He looks at me and grins, unless he's just showing his teeth. He's not as tall as his brother and only a few inches taller than me, so maybe he's not fully grown. Bears take five years to grow to maturity. I wonder where he goes to school, then decide he probably doesn't go anywhere. Bears probably home school. Otherwise, they'd have to go through several grades in a year, to make it come out right. I wonder how old I am in bear years, and if he's older than me.

VII. The Reception

Before she met with the caterer, Mom asked me, "For goodness' sake, what do bears eat?"

There are ham biscuits for the people and honey biscuits for the bears, melon soup for everybody. Trout with sauce and *au naturale*, as they say in French class. Raspberries. She didn't take my suggestion to serve the honey biscuits with dead bees. I'm sure the bears would have appreciated that.

The bears drink mead, which is made from honey. I try some. It feels like fire going down my throat, and burns like fire in my stomach. Like a fire on the altar of the Bear Goddess. Her name is Callisto. Once, by accident when she was hunting in the forest, she killed her son, Arcas. So she put him in a cave for the winter, and when spring came again, he emerged healed. That's why bears sleep through the winter.

This isn't what it says in *Bullfinch's Mythology*. But Catcher says Bullfinch got it all wrong. He says Bullfinch is a bunch of bull—. You know what I mean. He doesn't curse often, but when he does, Mom clutches the hem of her dress, as though trying to hold it against a wind that will lift it over her knees.

VIII. The Dancing

Dad doesn't remember how to dance, so he and Rosie sway back and forth, like teenagers at prom. The bears know how to dance, of course. They begin a Virginia Reel, whirling down the line in each other's arms, then go into figures I don't recognize. To punctuate the rhythm, they growl and stamp their feet.

Frog Biter asks me to dance. I guess he was checking me out, too, when the photographs were taken. I'm worried about following the bear dances, but he swings me out in a waltz. I never knew anyone could be so strong.

Yeah, he tells me. And I'm only four and a half. Wait until I'm fully grown. I'll be taller than Catcher.

Hearing this makes something burn in the pit of my stomach, which may be the mead.

IX. The Cake

Catcher cuts the cake, which is shaped like a beehive.
"What a charming couple they make," says Mrs. Ashby.

"I'm surprised she wore white," says Mrs. Coates. "I heard her relationship with the lawyer was pretty hot and heavy."

He feeds a slice to Rosie, then licks frosting from the corner of her mouth. His tongue is the color of raspberry ice cream.

"Do you think their children will be black?" asks Mrs. Mason, the minister's wife. She walks with a cane and must be over eighty.

"There are bears in the ladies' room," says Mrs. Partlow. "Do you know they go just like a man?"

"I think he's sexy, with all that fur," says Alison Coates. She's in my French class.

"I don't know how she caught him," says Mrs. Sutton. "All that real estate, and I never thought she was pretty in the first place."

She feeds him a slice. Her hand disappears into the darkness between his teeth.

X. The Honeymoon

Biter promises to stop whenever I want to.

When Rosie left on her honeymoon, everyone threw rose petals. They stuck to Catcher's fur. I could see her brushing them off through the limousine window.

It's nothing like when Eddie Tyler felt me up under the bleachers. His fur smells like rain, his mouth tastes like honey. I run my tongue over his incisors, and he laughs—or growls, I don't know which. And suddenly we're rolling around in the vestry, my fingers gripping his fur, trying to pull out brown tufts. It doesn't hurt him a bit.

I want to sleep with you, I say, and I mean through the winter, with the snow above us and branches covered with ice, creaking in the wind. While the deer are starving, searching for grasses under the snow, we'll lie next to each other, living off our fat, sharing body heat. I'll even cook him deer guts.

But he takes it another way, and that's all right too. His curved claws are good at climbing trees, and unbuttoning dresses. And I finally understand why my sister is marrying a bear. Maybe if Eddie Tyler had been a bear, I would have let him get to third base.

* * *

XI. The Announcement

Our June brides include Miss Rosalie Barlow, who was married in the First Methodist Church to Mr. T. C. Ursus. The new Mrs. Ursus has a B.A. from Sweet Briar College. Mr. Ursus manages his family's extensive property in the Blue Ridge Mountains. The maid of honor was Miss Blanche Barlow, the bride's sister. The best man was the groom's brother, Mr. F. B. Ursus. The bride carried white lilies and wore her mother's wedding dress of *peau de soie* decorated with seed pearls. The bride's mother, Mrs. Elwood Barlow, is the former Miss Buckingham County, 1965.

The Stepsister's Tale

It isn't easy, cutting into your feet.

Years later, when I had become a podiatrist,
I learned the parts of the feet. Did you know your feet
contain a quarter of your bones? Calcaneus, talus, cuboid, navicular.
Lateral, intermediate, and medial cuneiform.
Metatarsals and then the phalanges, proximal, middle, distal.
They're beautiful on the tongue, these words from a foreign language.

My sister cut into her heels, which are in the hindfoot.
I cut into my big toes, called the halluces.
She cut into flesh and tendon and sinew.
I cut into bone, between the phalanges,
through the interphalangeal joint.
That's in the forefoot, which bears half the body's weight.
To this day, both of us walk with a slight limp.

The problem is you do desperate things for love.
We loved her, the woman who wanted us to be perfect:
unblemished skin, waist like a corsetier's dream,
feet that would fit even the tiniest slipper.
And so we played the aristocratic game
of identify-the-princess.

Sometimes it's a slipper, sometimes a ring.
Oh mother, love me without asking me to scrape
my fingers like carrots, cut off my heels and toes.
Eventually, she became your favorite daughter,

the cinder-girl, the princess-designate.
She was the best at being perfect, but abuse
will do that to you.

A woman comes into my office, asking me
to cut off her little toes so she can wear
the latest fashion. I sit her down and say
did you know your feet provide the body
with balance, mobility, support?
Come, let me show you a model: here's the toe,
metatarsal and phalanges. You can see
how elegantly they move, as in a waltz,
surrounded by your blood vessels and nerves,
the ball gown of your soft tissue,
a protective coat of skin, the delicate nail.

Look, underneath, how beautiful you are . . .

The Clever Serving-Maid

Here are the things your mother did not give you:
a chest filled with linens for your marriage bed,
a casket of jewels to wear on your wedding day,
a handkerchief spotted with her own red blood,
a talking horse named Falada.

Here are the things she did: your life, of course,
a tendency to get in and out of trouble
since you were a scullion. And now here you are,
so grand, a lady's maid, but you are thinking
you could be grander still. So you tell the princess
to put on your plain brown linen while you dress
yourself in her sky-blue silk. It suits you better
anyway. And then you get on Falada.

The prince doesn't even notice the substitution.
Why should he? You've been in service since you were twelve.
You can sound as articulate as a duchess,
or more so, the way the butler is somehow always
more impressive than the king.

But you have to shake your head when you look out the window
and see her in the courtyard—the princess is hopeless
at tending geese. She'd make a terrible queen.
If she can't control a flock of geese, how can she
control a household, a diplomatic mission,
troops sent into battle? Queens have to know
these sorts of things, not just embroidery.

And look at the stable-boy pestering her! You would stick
your knife into him—then he'd stop being obnoxious!

You're sad when Falada dies, which wasn't your doing.
He was an old horse—what did anyone expect?
But the princess is inconsolable, cries all day,
her soft white hands are developing blisters, her nose
is getting freckled. All right you say, let's end
this charade. I'm not the princess.

The problem is, the prince has already fallen
in love with you, but he has a weak chin and eyes
like gooseberries. So you decide there's adventure
out there somewhere, countries you have not heard of,
seas that have not been sailed, another future
than either the one reserved for serving-maids
or princesses. As you walk through the castle gates
(the king is threatening to put you in a barrel
filled with nails and have you dragged through the streets
as punishment, the prince is begging you
to stay, the princess is looking confused, as always),
the head of Falada calls from above the gates,
"Where will you go, false maid?" You answer, "Anywhere
I please, and nowhere in particular."

The air is cool, the way it usually is
after a night of rain, the birds cacophonous.
The road winds through the town, then into forest.
Where should you go? East, you decide, where ahead of you
the sun has risen and shines on the dusty road,
making it seem, just for a moment, golden.

Seven Shoes

The witch said, "I will give you what you want.
All you have to do is wear through seven
pairs of shoes." "Which shoes?" she asked. "Oh, any.
But the number is important."

The first pair, she was wearing that day in the woods:
red Keds. In them, she would ride her bike down the road,
hike along the top of the ridge to a tree
where an owl was nesting, wade through the rocky stream,
until her mother declared they were beyond help.
But each time, they revived in the washing machine.
She would wear them to go hunting for dragonflies
and minnows, or up to the attic where she kept
her favorite books. Finally, the soles split
while she was climbing over slick, wet rocks.
She almost fell into the muddy water,
not that she would have minded.
By then, they had faded to a dusty pink.

The second was a pair of flip-flops bought
for a dollar at the bait and tackle shop
next to the lake while visiting her father.
By the end of summer, they were getting moldy
from all the times she had worn them in the canoe,
rowing along the banks through lotus flowers,
leaving a path of dark water in her wake.
Finally, on a fishing trip, the strap
broke, and she walked back barefoot,
carrying the trout in a basket, almost sorry

it would be her dinner that night,
with butter and parsley.

The third was a pair of silver sandals, worn
to the spring formal with a long blue dress
the color of the sky that reminded her
of both Amelia Earhart and a princess.
They only lasted an hour: the buckle snapped.
After that, she danced barefoot in the gym,
holding hands with her friends under basketball hoops
decorated with paper streamers.

The fourth was a pair of black patent pumps she wore
to her law firm internship, running up and down
the internal staircase, taking notes at meetings,
sitting in on conference calls, making copies.
One day, while she was hurrying to the deli
to pick up sandwiches, her left heel caught
between two bricks of an ancient city sidewalk.
She twisted her ankle and laddered her pantyhose.
The patent leather cracked.

The fifth was a pair of sensible boots that lasted
through four New England winters while she trudged
along a familiar track from dorm to classrooms
to library, and back.
By the time she graduated, the leather tops
had separated from the rubber soles,
so water seeped through and soaked both layers of socks.
But the degree was worth wet feet.

The sixth pair were white satin and cost as much
as her dress, which she had found in a second-hand store,
real silk, probably from the 1950s.
She danced in them carefully, they felt so delicate,
and made her feel delicate too. Later, she wrapped them
in tissue paper and stored them beside the veil
of antique lace, the bouquet of silk roses.

They were shoes for just one day. As in a fairy tale,
they had served their purpose.

The seventh was a pair of bedroom slippers.
She wore through the soles by walking back and forth
in the apartment until her daughter was sleeping.
Then she would sit at her desk beside the crib
and work on her dissertation while the words
swam in front of her eyes, she was so tired.
Like minnows in a stream... She wondered where
that image had come from. One day, she realized the slippers
had worn right through: there were holes under her toes.
She had not even noticed.

By then, she had forgotten the witch in the woods.
One day, as she was walking through the campus
where she was now a professor, she met a woman
who asked, "So, have you started writing your stories?"
"Sort of," she said, wondering how this person,
dressed in a raincoat, with a colorful kerchief
over her head, very Eastern European,
knew that late at night when the papers were graded
and her daughter had gone to bed after finishing homework,
she would sit at her computer, trying to write.
That morning she had put on a pair of red Keds
that for some reason always made her happy,
even though the weather channel had forecast rain.
"I'm working on a novel," she replied.
"I've always wanted to be a writer, since
I was a little girl." "Good," said the woman,
patting her on the arm. "You're ready now."

The Other Thea

Thea stared out the train window. Forest, more forest, and then a small town would flash by. And then more forest. She had taken this route many times while she was in school, although then she's traveled with a large trunk filled with the clothes and books she would need for a semester at Miss Lavender's. This time she had a backpack, with just enough for a day or two. How long would it take? She hadn't really known what to bring. Should she even be going, in the middle of Winter Break?

But she hadn't known what else to do. She checked the text on her phone: *Of course. Always pleased to see you, Thea. Let us know when your train gets in. Love, Emily*

Then a smiling black cat emoji. It was not one of the regular iPhone emoji, but Thea was not surprised that Miss Gray had somehow gotten into her phone. After all, she taught *Magic and Technology.* Thea remembered her standing in front of the classroom: "Manipulating technology is no different from manipulating any other aspect of reality," she had said. And then she had put some complicated equations up on the board. Math was Thea's least favorite part of magic. The poetry part had always come more naturally to her.

And then her text in response: *Arriving Thursday 2 p.m. I'll walk from the station.*

Miss Gray's response was another black cat emoji. It winked at her.

"Next stop, Miss," said the conductor. She looked up, startled. "Aren't you one of Miss Lavender's girls?"

"I was," said Thea. "I graduated last year."

He nodded. "Thought I remembered you, with that ginger hair." He pronounced it *jin-juh.* "If you need help with anything, let me know."

"Thanks," she said, and smiled. It was a weak smile, she knew that. She hadn't been very good at smiling lately.

"Hartfield, Massachusetts!" he called down the train corridor. "Next stop Hartfield!"

Thea put her phone back in her backpack and zipped up her jacket. She made her way to the end of the compartment.

Forest, more forest. And then the first houses of Hartfield, with weatherbeaten wooden siding. Suddenly they were in the town center, with its brick dental offices, boutiques, and coffee shops. The train slowed, then pulled into the station. The conductor put a metal bridge over the gap, and Thea walked across it. Here she was again, not for some sort of alumnae event, but because she didn't know where else to go.

From the station, she walked up Main Street, passing several antiques stores, the food co-op, and Booktopia, where students from Miss Lavender's always congregated on Saturdays, ordering cappuccinos and egg or chicken salad sandwiches, reading Sylvia Plath or Margaret Atwood or the latest Kelly Link. Should she stop in for a moment? Maybe . . .

Before she could reconsider, she had stepped inside, and there was Sam at the counter. She had not expected him to be, well, right there.

"Thea," he said, a wide smile spreading over his face. It was accepted wisdom at Miss Lavender's that Sam looked like a frog. Nevertheless, a respectable percentage of the students admitted to having crushes on him, despite or because of his rumpled hair, flannel shirts, and encyclopedic knowledge of literature. He had been a clerk at the bookstore through high school. During Thea's sophomore year he had left for college, but his mother had been diagnosed with cancer, and since his parents were divorced, he had returned to Hartfield to care for her. After her death, he had bought Booktopia with the insurance. As he reminded the town council on a regular basis, every town needed an independent bookstore. Now he was finishing his degree by taking night classes at UMass Amherst. At least that's what it had said on the Booktopia blog, the last time Thea had checked.

"What are you doing back here? Don't you live in Boston now? Wait, I'll make you a cappuccino."

"No, that's OK, they're expecting me. But thanks. Yeah, Boston. I'm starting college next fall. I think. I mean, I am. I just took a gap year, that's all. I figured I'd stop in here for a minute, you know, to check out the writing books." There was a special section right up front, left over from National Novel Writing Month, with everything from *The Elements of Style* to Anne Lamott. "And to see where we used to hang out."

His eyes crinkled up at the corners. "Aren't you a little young to be getting nostalgic? You only graduated six months ago."

"Yeah." Thea laughed uncomfortably. "Way too young. Well, I'd better be going. They're expecting me. Maybe I'll come back . . . for one of those books. I always meant to read John Gardner."

"If you have time, come back and tell me about your life in the big city. I'll give you a sandwich on the house. Or, to be more accurate, on the store."

"Yeah, all right, thanks." She turned, then pushed the door open again. Standing outside in the cold air, she thought, *God, I am such a dork.*

He hadn't changed at all. Of course, people didn't change that much in six months. Except her. She had changed, in ways she didn't understand. That was why she had come back here. She continued up Main Street, then turned down Oak and Maple (seriously, how unimaginative were the people who named streets in small New England towns?). And there, at the edge of town, were the brick main house and buildings of Miss Lavender's. And the familiar sign:

Miss Lavender's School of Witchcraft
Founded 1812

Thea had never seen the grounds looking so deserted. The last time she had been here, she had been graduating, and the town had been filled with students and their parents.

Not hers, of course. Her parents had died when she was a child, and her grandmother had been sick for many years—far too sick to travel, for parents' weekends or even graduation. At those sorts of events, one or another friend's parents had always temporarily adopted her, and she had felt what it would be like to have a family, for a little while.

She walked up to the main house, which held the headmistress's office. She rang the bell and heard it echoing through the building.

"So you're back." She looked around, but saw no one. "Down here, idiot."

She looked down. "Oh, it's you, Cordelia. Hello." The tortoise-shell tabby stared up at her with yellow eyes.

"Hello yourself. I'm not at all surprised to see you again."

Before Thea could ask why, the door opened and there was Mrs. Moth, looking just as she always did, in a respectable wool skirt and cardigan, gray hair a little messy as though she had been running her fingers through it. The image of a headmistress.

"Thea, it's so good to see you," she said. "Do come in. I've just made tea. And you," she said, looking down at the cat. "You could have told us you would be out all night. You know how Lavinia worries."

"I was out on cat business, which is none of your business," said Cordelia. She slipped around Mrs. Moth's ankles and disappeared down the hallway.

"Cats!" said Mrs. Moth, shaking her head. "Come in, my dear. Let's go into the parlor. I've prepared one of the guest rooms for you. I'm afraid everyone's gone for the break—it's just me, Lavinia, and Emily right now. We always give teachers and staff two weeks for the holidays."

Sure enough, when Thea went into the parlor, where Mrs. Moth usually met with prospective students and their parents, there was Miss Lavender sitting on the sofa. Whereas Mrs. Moth was comfortably plump, Lavinia Lavender was thin and angular. She was wearing a soft gray dress, and the white hair escaping from her bun formed a halo around her face. It would have been intimidating, having tea with the founder of the school, but Miss Lavender looked so perfectly harmless. She was so forgetful that she sometimes accidentally walked through walls. It was a good thing that Mrs. Moth had taken over as headmistress, long before any of the alumnae could remember. But older students who had taken her seminar on *Philosophy of Magic* warned younger ones not to underestimate Miss Lavender. How could you be expected to remember the locations of walls when you were contemplating the fundamental structure of reality?

And standing beside the fireplace was Miss Emily Gray. Thea was almost shocked to see that she was wearing leggings and a loose sweater, as though she had just finished doing yoga or something. Her brown hair hung in a neat braid over one shoulder. It made Miss Gray seem almost human, although as soon as she said "Hello, Thea. It's so nice to see you again," Thea mentally panicked at the thought that she might have forgotten to do her homework. Did she look a mess? She was sure that she looked a mess. She took a deep breath.

"Cookies on the table, and I'll bring the tea," said Mrs. Moth, then disappeared down the hall toward the kitchen.

Thea quailed at the thought of having to make small talk with Miss Lavender and Miss Gray, but she should have known better. Witches don't make small talk.

"So what's the matter?" asked Miss Gray, sitting down on the sofa beside Miss Lavender. "You wouldn't have called if there was nothing wrong."

Thea put her backpack down and sat in one of the comfortable armchairs. While she was gathering her thoughts, trying to figure out what to say, Mrs. Moth came in with the tea things.

"Orange Pekoe for Lavinia," she said. "Oolong for Emily, and Earl Gray for me. Thea, I'm guessing you want a chai latte. You'll have to add milk." There was nothing in the cups when she poured out, but out of the teapot came four distinctly different smells and colors of tea. Thea added milk and sugar to her cup, then stirred.

"The thing is, I'm not sure," she said. "You know my grandmother died last summer, just after graduation. Thanks for the wreath, by the way. She would have really liked getting a wreath from the school. That was tough, but at first I was all right. I mean, we were never close or anything. I had to meet with her lawyer, then catalog all her furniture for the auction. I sold almost everything, except Mom's stuff. And then I had to sell the house. After that . . . I was supposed to be at Harvard this fall. But I just couldn't—I don't know, I was so tired. So I deferred for a year, and I rented an apartment in Boston. I figured I'd write . . . . you know, start becoming a great writer." She smiled self-deprecatingly, in case they thought she was being too grandiose, although all through school that had been her talent: senior year, to her surprise, she had been chosen editor-in-chief of *The Broomstick*. "But I couldn't do that either. So I've been living in the apartment, doing—nothing, really. Some days I just wander around the city. Some days I don't even get out of my pajamas." Thea put her head down in her hands. "I don't know what's wrong with me."

Miss Gray took a sip of her tea. "When you went through your grandmother's house, did you find your shadow?"

It was the question she'd been dreading. When she'd first arrived at school, Mrs. Moth had sent a letter to her grandmother:

Dear Mrs. Tillinghast,
Thea seems to have forgotten her shadow. Since she will need
it to participate fully in school activities, could you please
send it as soon as possible?
        With best regards,
        Wilhelmina Moth, Headmistress

A week later, she had received a reply:

Dear Mrs. Moth,
As Thea may have told you, several years ago Mrs. Tilling-
hast suffered a stroke. Although she has recovered a great
deal, she lost some of her long-term memory and fine motor
coordination, which is why I am writing this letter for her.
She says she remembers putting Thea's shadow in a box, but
doesn't remember where she put the box. She says it was a
very troublesome shadow, and Thea is better off without it.
I'm sorry not to be more helpful, and please give my love to
Thea.
        Respectfully yours,
        Anne Featherstone, Mrs. Tillinghast's secretary

It had happened when she was six. After both of her parents
died when their small plane went down, Thea had been sent to live
with her grandmother. She had hated the gloomy old house, and the
gloomy old woman who told her that her mother should never have
married that spendthrift, good-for-nothing Michael Graves. If she
hadn't, she would not be dead now.

One day, after her grandmother had forbidden her from going
out into the garden, she had shouted, "I hate you! You're not my
mother. I'm going to run away and you'll never see me again, you
old bitch!" Her grandmother had ordered the butler to hold her, and
with a pair of gardening shears she had cut off Thea's shadow, *snip
snip*. And that was the last Thea had seen of it. By the time her grandmother sent her to Miss Lavender's, the third generation to attend,
she had almost forgotten it wasn't there.

"Most people don't even notice," she had said to Mrs. Moth
when first asked about it. She had just arrived at Miss Lavender's,
and was trying to figure out where her room was, what classes she

would be taking, whether she would fit in or have friends. It was so different from her middle school in Virginia.

"Most people aren't witches," Mrs. Moth had replied. "While you're here, we'll work around it, but there will be certain kinds of magic you can't do. And you'll need it eventually."

Sometimes new students had said, "What's wrong with Thea? Why doesn't she have a shadow?" But at Miss Lavender's one quickly learned that if one's roommate turned into a wolf at certain times of the month, or was faintly, almost imperceptibly green, or was missing a shadow, it was considered impolite to remark on it as anything extraordinary.

Before she had left for her grandmother's funeral, Miss Gray had said to her, "Find your shadow, Thea. It's time." Well, she had tried.

"No," she said now, in response to Miss Gray's question. "I looked everywhere," from the attic to the cellar, with Anne and the butler and cook until they were all covered with dust, "but I couldn't find it. I have no idea what happened to it. Do you think that's what's wrong with me?"

"Of course, my dear," said Miss Lavender, speaking for the first time. "You could do without it as a child, but now that you're a grown woman—well, a grown woman needs her shadow. Without it, you're fading."

Fading? She was fading?

"It's part of growing up," said Mrs. Moth. "Children don't need their shadows, strictly speaking—remember Peter Pan. But adults are a different matter. Lavinia's right, without it you'll fade away. It will take some time, but I'm afraid the process has already begun. Eventually even ordinary people—well, not ordinary of course, but not witches—will start to notice. Let's just see if we can find it, shall we? This didn't work the last time we tried—I suspect the box was shielded with a spell of some sort. But since your grandmother's passed away and the box has been lost . . . perhaps, just perhaps, it will work now."

How could she be fading? But Miss Lavender, more than anyone, could see things other people couldn't. In school, it was rumored that she could even see the futures—the multiple possibilities created by each moment.

Mrs. Moth leaned down and blew on Thea's tea. In the teacup, on the milky brown liquid, she saw an image form, in sepia like an old photograph. A castle with strange, twisting spires, and mountains in the distance.

"I've seen that before," she said.

"Of course you have," said Miss Gray. "We went there on an eleventh-grade field trip."

Then it must be . . . "Mother Night's castle. Is that where my shadow went?"

"Yes," said Mrs. Moth. "And I'm afraid you'll need to go find it. You can't do without it much longer. When Lavinia says fading, she doesn't just mean visually. Without it, you'll keep getting more tired. You'll start feeling despondent, as though you'll never accomplish anything. Eventually, it will seem too difficult even to try. One day you might not get up at all."

"But how can I find it?" asked Thea. "Mother Night's castle is in the Other Country. When we went, Miss Gray took us. Can you take me there again?" She looked at Miss Gray.

The teacher shook her head so that her brown braid swung around.

"Thea, my dear," said Mrs. Moth, "you are a graduate of this school. Like any witch, you should be able to find your way to the Other Country. By yourself."

The next morning, Thea woke to Cordelia patting her nose.

"Stop that," she said, and rolled over. That's right, she was at Miss Lavender's, in a guest bedroom on the second floor of the head-mistress's house. Through the window, she could see the dormitory where she had spent six years of her life. It reminded her that Shosha-na had sent her a Facebook message a couple of days ago, asking if Thea was all right and complaining about Chem 101. Of her two se-nior-year suitemates, Shoshana Washington was pre-med at Brown, and Lily Yu was in China working for a human rights organization. She would start an Asian Literature and Culture major at Stanford in the fall. She kept posting pictures of dumplings and rainy green hills on Instagram. Thea really should keep up with them, but it was hard when she was the only one who had nothing to say. *Binge-watched Netflix and ate ice cream for dinner* didn't make for a very inspiring Facebook post.

"Are you getting up, or do I have to sit on your face?"

She turned back over. "Cordy, how do you get to the Other Country?"

"How do I get there? I'm a cat—I just go. The question is, how do you get there?" All cats knew the way to the Other Country. That was one of the first lessons in *Care and Feeding of a Familiar*. If you couldn't find your cat, it was probably in the Other Country.

Thea scratched the cat behind her ears. "Can't you just take me there?"

"No, I can't take you. A little lower down . . . there. Now under the chin." For a moment, Cordelia actually purred. Then she continued, "You're a thick, clumsy human. You can't go the way cats go. We just slip between things. You need to go through a door."

"I remember!" said Thea. "When we went in eleventh grade, it was through a door. And the door was in this house . . . But I don't remember which one it was. Cordy, can you show me which door goes to the Other Country?"

Cordelia swatted her hand away and looked at her with contempt. "Now you really are being an idiot. After six years in this place, you should at least know how to think like a witch."

Think like a witch? What did the cat mean? Suddenly she remembered a visiting lecturer, an alumna named Dr. Something Patel who taught physics at one of the local universities. She had come to talk to Miss Gray's class about magical physics. Thea remembered her standing in front of the blackboard, chalk in hand, saying . . . how did it go? "One of the most important things I learned in my time at Miss Lavender's, which has served me well as a theoretical physicist, is to think like a witch. If you can't find the answer, a witch would say, you're probably asking the wrong question." Miss Gray had nodded emphatically.

Think like a witch.

"It's not *the* door. It's *a* door. I'm going to take a shower. I'll be ready in ten minutes. Wait for me, okay?"

Cordelia didn't answer. She stretched out in a sunny spot on the coverlet and started to wash herself.

Twenty minutes later, Thea was ready. In her backpack, she had a change of clothes, toiletries zipped into plastic bags, a notebook and pens, a battered copy of *A Wrinkle in Time* that she had been rereading, and half a chocolate bar.

"Are you coming?" she said to Cordelia. "Or did you wake me up this morning just because you felt like it?"

"I'm coming." The cat jumped down from the bed, then looked up at her. "Which door?"

"Kitchen. That way I can grab some breakfast along the way."

Thea walked quietly in case anyone else was still asleep, down the back stairs and to the kitchen. Last night, Mrs. Moth had shown her where everything was kept. "Just make yourself breakfast anytime you like," she had said. Thea found a bagel, then cream cheese to smear on both sides. She put them together to form a sandwich so it would be easier to carry. She put an apple into her backpack. That would have to do.

"All right," she said, holding the bagel in one hand, with the backpack slung over her shoulder. "Let's see if I'm right about how to do this."

She walked to the kitchen door. Standing in front of it, she took the notebook out of her backpack, scribbled a few lines . . . Then she put her hand on the door handle and read,

"An entrance, entranced,
you open into the brightness
of summer and winter dancing,
white snow on white blossoms,
in the country of my longing."

Not her best effort, but perhaps it would do. And she did like the pun: entrance, entranced. The trick was to tell the door what it was, what it could become. "The creation speaks two languages," Miss Gray had told them in *Introduction to Magical Rhetoric*. "Poetry and math, which are the same language to anyone who speaks them correctly. You must speak to the creation in its own language, so it understands what you want it to do." Thea took a deep breath, hoping the spell had worked, and opened the door.

It was summer. It is always summer in the Other Country, or rather it is always no season at all: the apple trees are always blossoming, and in leaf, and bearing fruit at the same time. Sometimes it snows, and white flakes settle on the ripening fruit. But today seemed to be a perfect summer day. Thea and Cordelia walked down the sloping green hill toward the castle. Tall grass brushed against Thea's jeans, and the sun was warm enough that she stopped for a moment to take off her jacket and stuff it into her backpack. Beyond the castle was a lake, shining in the sunlight, and beyond the lake were mountains with forested slopes and snowy peaks. It looked like a postcard, or something that had been Photoshopped.

The last time she had been here, Shoshana had squealed in delight and Lily had said, "Seriously, are you making that noise? Because stop." Miss Gray had said, "Come on, girls. We're on a schedule." The castle looked just as Thea remembered—beautiful, but strange. As she and Cordelia walked down the hill and came to the gardens, she could see more clearly the stone towers, some going straight up and covered with small balconies, some spiraling like a narwhal's horn, some curled like a snail's shell. The buttresses, some of them supporting nothing but air, resembled a whale's skeleton. The whole structure was improbable, like a castle out of a dream, and reminded Thea of an Escher print. One of those towers, probably the largest, held the Tapestry Room, where gold spiders with jeweled eyes crawled up and down, weaving the threads of life into an enormous tapestry, whose front no person had ever seen. Her thread was somewhere in there. She wondered what it looked like, which part of the pattern it formed.

"And this," she remembered Miss Gray saying, in a voice like a tour guide's, "is the Library of Lost Books. All the books that are lost in the worlds are kept here. To our left, you will see the extension built specifically after the burning of the Library of Alexandria."

Thea stepped onto a garden path. Cordelia ran ahead and stood by the side of a long stone pool with yellow lotus flowers at its farther edge.

"Something interesting?" asked Thea.

"Fish," said the cat, staring down intently.

Thea sat on a stone bench beside the path and put her backpack next to her. She was starting to feel hot, and the bench was shaded by a linden tree, both blossoming and in leaf. "Anyway, I need a plan, you know," she said.

"Why?" said Cordelia, reaching a paw tentatively into the water.

"Well, because I need to find my shadow, and then I need to take it back with me, and I don't know how to do either of those things, is why." What she really wanted to do was stay here, in the warmth and sunlight, with the sound of bees buzzing in the linden flowers above her. After all, she had no idea how to find her shadow, or what to do after she had found it. She would sit, just for a little while . . . At least it was better than sitting in her apartment, scrolling aimlessly through her Facebook newsfeed.

Cordelia leaned down and patted at the water, then jumped back, shaking her head from side to side.

"That's right, stupid cat!" came a shrill voice. "If you put your head down here, I'll spit at you again!" Thea leaned forward just enough to see an orange head sticking out of the water. One of the fish, looking rather pleased with itself. Thea heard a clucking sound and realized that it was laughing. Then it disappeared back beneath the green surface of the water. Cordelia hastily licked herself all over and then stalked off along the path, as though nothing had happened.

"Hey, where are you going?" Thea called, but the cat did not turn back or answer. She was alone in the still, sunlit garden.

"I want my ball back, and I want it now!"

She turned in the direction of the voice. A girl about her own age was walking toward her, dressed in a bathing suit that looked as though it had come from the 1930s, with a frilled bathing cap on her head. "Where is it, Thea? I swear, if you don't give it to me right now, I'm going to turn you into a toad, or worse!"

Thea stared at her in astonishment. The girl pulled off her bathing cap, and down fell long black hair, with stars tangled in it. "Seriously, I don't know why my mother puts up with you. If I were her, I'd put you back in that box!"

"Lady Morgan?" said Thea, hesitantly. This must be Mother Night's daughter. Was she supposed to curtsey or something? They had not met her on the field trip, but who else would be walking around the castle gardens as though she owned them, talking about her mother? And what was that about a box? "I'm not Thea. I mean, I'm the other Thea. I mean, she's the other Thea—I'm the real one."

"Oh!" said Morgan Morningstar, looking at her with astonishment. "Why, so you are. You're faded around the edges. Well for goodness' sake take her back with you—she's such a pest. You'd think being in a box for twelve years would have calmed her down, but evidently not. Last week, she almost started a fire in the library—there's a reason that fireplace is never used! She and one of those annoying satyrs thought it would be a good place to toast marshmallows. Can you imagine? Now that you're here, you can take her—where are you from, anyway?"

"Miss Lavender's," said Thea. She stood up, but decided not to curtsey. The time had passed for it, anyhow.

"Oh, how nice. Say hello to Emily and Mina and dear old Lavinia for me. You must be one of the students."

I graduated, Thea wanted to tell her, but Morgan had already taken her arm and was pulling her down the path toward the castle. "The problem is finding her. She stole my Seeing Ball, and now she can see me coming and hide. You know a shadow can hide in very small places, and the castle has lots of those. But now that you're here, maybe we can convince Mom to send her back. It's clear that Thea—the other Thea—should go home with you. I mean, look at you . . ."

Thea didn't know how to respond, but she didn't have to. Morgan Morningstar was pulling her through the gardens: between flowering borders, and through a privet maze that Thea would surely have gotten lost in, and over a lawn laid out like a checkerboard, with chamomile forming the white squares. Where had Cordelia gone? Drat all cats. Then they were in the castle courtyard, with its Egyptian and Greek and Indian statues, and through the arched doorway.

The great hall was cool and dim after the sunlit courtyard. Just as she remembered, it had no ceiling: tall pillars ascended up to the blue sky. But the sun was already sinking toward the mountains, so the hall was mostly in shadow. It was empty except for a small group of people at the far end, close to the dais.

"Mom!" Morgan called. "Look who I found by the lotus pool."

Several of the—people?—stepped back. Thea noticed a man with the antlers of a stag, a woman with ivy growing over her head instead of hair, and a woman who looked exactly like Dr. Patel, only what would Dr. Patel be doing here? A pirate, in a black leather coat and tricorne hat, took off his hat and bowed to her. But between them all was Mother Night. Today she looked like her daughter, black hair falling to her feet, a face as pale as the moon, unlined. She could have been Morgan's twin. The last time Thea had seen her, she had looked immensely old, with gray hair that wound around her head like a coronet. She had been sitting on her throne, and Miss Gray had introduced the Miss Lavender's students to her, one by one. They had bobbed awkward curtseys, having learned how to curtsey just the week before. Thea remembered what Miss Gray had told them: "Don't be nervous, but remember that she created the universe." It didn't matter what she looked like at any particular moment. You couldn't mistake Mother Night.

"Mom, this is . . ."

"I know, sweetheart. Hello, Thea. We've been expecting you. How are you feeling?"

"Pretty well, Ma'am," said Thea, doing her best to curtsey, trying to remember how. This time she was sure she should curtsey.

"How do you think she's feeling?" said Morgan. "Look at her. Soon she'll be as transparent as a ghost. I could poke my finger through her, not that I want to. You need to make Thea—I mean shadow Thea—go back with her."

"Your mother doesn't *need* to do anything," said the pirate. But he said it so charmingly, with a grin and a wink at Thea, that she could not help smiling back at him. "I know you're in a bad mood, Morgan . . ."

"Don't you start with me, Raven," said Morgan, still gripping Thea by the arm. "You said the same thing when she stole your cloak of invisibility. You said, 'That shadow has to go.' Remember?"

So this was Raven! The famous, or infamous, Raven . . . Mother Night's consort.

"Stop, both of you," said Mother Night. "I can't make her go, for the simple reason that while she's separated from Thea, she's a person. Like any of you. Like Thea herself. I will not order her to leave here. I'm sorry, my dear," she said to Thea. "You need to figure this out yourself." Which was just what Mrs. Moth had told her. Thea felt sick to her stomach. She had no idea how to find her shadow, much less convince her to . . . what, exactly? She still wasn't sure. And what had Morgan meant—as transparent as a ghost? Was she fading that fast?

"Remember there's a ball tonight," Mother Night continued. "The other Thea will certainly be there—she loves to dance. And now, I have some things to attend to before the ball."

"I'll come with you," said Raven, taking her by the arm. The antlered man and the ivy-haired woman followed them out, as did Dr. Patel before Thea could say hello as a fellow Miss Lavender's alum.

"He always takes her side," said Morgan. "I guess I can't blame him. They've been together for what, a thousand years? But I really wanted Mom to just *do* something for once."

"So where do you think we'll find her?" asked Thea. "The shadow, I mean."

"Oh, Mom's right. She'll be at the ball. She wouldn't miss a party, and I have to admit, she is a good dancer. Come on, we need to find clothes to wear. We can't go to the ball looking like this—at least, you can't."

Thea looked down at her jeans and gray Gap shirt. No, she couldn't. Could Morgan really have put a finger through her? She looked solid enough. Tentatively, she poked herself in the stomach. She felt solid. But both Morgan and Mrs. Moth had talked about her fading at the edges, slowly becoming transparent. She wished she didn't have to worry so much—about herself, and the shadow Thea. She was going to a ball in Mother Night's castle! Shoshana was going to freak out. Even Lily might be impressed. Which reminded her . . .

As she followed Morgan down a series of twisting stone hallways, she took out her iPhone. No reception here, of course, but she could take photos and share them later with Shoshana and Lily in their private Facebook group.

Morgan's room was the entire top of a tower. Out of a large wardrobe, she drew dresses and suits of silk and velvet and lace, tossing them on her bed, which was shaped like a swan with its neck curved to form a backboard, while Thea walked around, looking through all the windows. Below she could see the castle and gardens. In one direction, hills and fields stretched away into the distance, until she could see a darkness that must be the sea. In the other, the lake reflected the setting sun, which was just beginning to touch the tops of the mountains with pink and orange.

"What else is there besides the castle?" asked Thea. "I mean, we only ever visited here. Are there—towns in the Other Country? If I went out there, what would I find?"

"All the stories you ever heard of," said Morgan. "And a whole lot you haven't. What about this?" *This* was a dress of green velvet that looked as though it had come from a museum exhibit or a Hollywood red carpet. "You can wear it with this." The second *this* was a mask of peacock feathers. Morgan rummaged among the clothes she had thrown on the bed.

"What are you going to wear?" asked Thea.

Morgan held up a black leather coat just like Raven's, and put a hat just like his on her head. "With this," she said, holding a mask of black feathers to her face. The smile beneath it was mocking.

"You're still mad at him, aren't you?"

"I just don't like him telling me what to do. He's not my father. And he's, what, as old as civilization itself? That's nothing." Morgan shrugged. "That's like a moment in time."

"But your mother also said . . ."

"Well yeah, Mom. That's different. But Mom's never stopped me from doing anything I want to. She doesn't, you know—interfere. She knows what's on the front of the tapestry, the fate of every person in every world as it's being woven. Sometimes I wish she would step in and act, especially when you otherworlders are doing something dreadful, like having another war. But she says that's what we're here for—you and me and Emily Gray. We're the ones responsible for changing things. That's why places like Miss Lavender's exist. Come on, it's getting dark. You can get dressed in the bathroom."

When Thea emerged from what turned out to be a surprisingly normal bathroom—but she figured people in Mother Night's castle needed to pee just like everyone else—she looked as though she had stepped out of a painting. Green velvet fell to the floor, covering her red Keds. Morgan's shoes had all been too small for her.

"I suppose you could magic your feet smaller," said Morgan, but at the beginning of junior year Mrs. Moth had told Thea's class, "If I discover that any of you have used magic for such a vain, trivial purpose as changing your physical dimensions, you will come to my office and have a serious talk with me." That had been enough to deter experimentation. Anyway, Thea wanted to feel at least a little like herself, underneath the dress and mask.

Before they left, she took two selfies in the wardrobe mirror: one by herself and one with the Morningstar, in which Morgan held up two fingers in a peace sign. What would Lily and Shoshana think of *that*? And then she followed Morgan back down through the castle corridors, passing what were obviously partygoers because they wore black tie or fantastical robes and gowns. Most of them wore masks, although sometimes she could not tell whether the masks were simply their faces.

In the great hall, it was twilight. The moon hung directly overhead, surrounded by constellations Thea did not recognize. The hall was illuminated by bubbles of light that floated through the air, seemingly wherever they wished. Earlier the hall had been bare stone, but now between the columns grew a forest of slender birch trees, with leaves that shone silver in the light of the floating bubbles. Thea reached up to touch a leaf and found that it was, indeed, made of pliable metal.

Beneath this forest moved the strangest, most fantastical people Thea had ever seen. There was the stag man, with flowers draped over his antlers. A woman with scaled blue skin was talking to what looked like a large owl. Three young girls with pig snouts were slipping in and out between the trees, playing tag. A satyr was bowing to a woman whose dress seemed to be made of butterflies—not just bowing, but asking her to dance, because now the music was starting. The butterflies fluttered as she took his hand. In the center of the hall was a dance floor that looked like a forest glade, with mossy rocks at its edges to sit on. A small stream ran through it, so dancers had to be nimble to avoid stepping in the water.

"I'll take it as a compliment." Thea turned around. There was Raven, looking Morgan up and down critically. "You could be me as a beardless boy, a thousand years ago."

"I don't think I'll be mistaken for you tonight," said Morgan, then burst out laughing. But who could blame her? The dashing pirate of that afternoon now had the head of a fox, with the same expression of sly humor under the tricorne hat. "Are you showing your true face, Monsieur Renard?"

"One of them, at any rate. *Hola*, I hear a sarabande! Shall we dance, Lady Morgan?"

"I'll be back," said Morgan to Thea. "The refreshments table is over against the wall. You'll be all right, right?" Thea barely had time to nod before Morgan was swept away by the fox man. She took off her mask, which felt hot and strange. What was she doing here anyway? Suddenly, she felt lost and alone.

"How are you, my dear?" Thea turned toward the voice—it was Mother Night. She looked completely different than she had that afternoon. Now her skin was dark, almost blue-black, and she had a nimbus of short white curls around her head. She was wearing a silver dress, very simply cut, that could have come from ancient Egypt or a modern fashion magazine.

"I'm all right, I guess," said Thea. But she didn't feel all right. Instead, she felt as though she might throw up.

"You haven't eaten anything since breakfast, not even the apple in your backpack. You forgot about it, didn't you? You have half a chocolate bar in there too, in the front pocket. So of course you're going to feel sick. You need to take better care of yourself."

"I'm not very good at that," said Thea. "Taking care of myself, I mean."

"No, you're not. But you don't have anyone else to do it, so you'll have to get better at it. Why don't you practice right now? Go over to the refreshments table and get yourself some of the fish pie, which is very good. And there's asparagus with hollandaise, and ice cream. But meat and vegetables first! Not just ice cream, you know." Thea nodded. It had been a long time since anyone had told her to eat healthily, and the fact that Mother Night was doing it made her feel like laughing, despite her sense of nausea.

"I'm serious," said Mother Night. She put her hands, cool and dry, on either side of Thea's face. Her eyes were black, with stars in them. For a moment, Thea felt as though she were floating in space. "Try to remember that you're also one of my daughters." And then, with a soft pat on the cheek, of both affection and admonition, Mother Night was gone. Thea shook her head as though to clear it, then walked around the dance floor, weaving between the birch trees and mossy stones, stepping over the stream, to the refreshments table.

She hung the peacock mask over her arm by its ribbons, then took a plate and some cutlery that looked like forks and knives on one end, and birch branches on the other. That must be fish pie—at least the crust was baked in the shape of a fish. She did not like asparagus but took some anyway, as well as some scalloped potatoes. A potato was a vegetable, right?

"What do you think that is?" asked the person ahead of her in line. Suddenly, she realized who she had been standing behind.

"Dr. Patel?" she said. The professor was wearing an ordinary black evening dress, with pearls. "I don't know, it looks sort of like a fern, you know those fiddle-head ferns they sell at the farmer's market, except those aren't usually purple, are they? I'm Thea Graves. I graduated from Miss Lavender's last spring. I think you lectured to one of my classes. On magic and physics?"

"Oh, hello," said Dr. Patel, smiling the way people do when they're trying to remember who you are. "Call me Anita. It's always nice to see a fellow alumna. Have you tried those little cakes? The ones in all different shapes and colors. They have marzipan inside."

Thea took several of the cakes. She did like marzipan. "It's weird seeing someone I know—I mean, sort of know—here in the Other Country. Are you . . . just visiting?"

"Wouldn't that be nice!" said Dr. Patel. "Sometimes I think only students get real vacations. No, I'm afraid that I'm here on business . . . Mother Night's business, of course. And you?"

"Oh, um, yeah. Me too, business."

"Emily used to say, *We are all on Mother Night's business, no matter what we're doing.* I bet she still says that to her students. How is everyone at Miss Lavender's? It's been so long since I visited—Homecoming, I think."

Suddenly, Thea had a vision of Miss Emily Gray, and Dr. Patel, and Morgan Morningstar, all going about Mother Night's business, whatever that might be.

"I'm really just here to find my shadow," she confessed. She didn't want Dr. Patel to think that she was taking too much credit, making her business out to be grander than it was . . .

"Unless it finds you first!"

Thea turned around. There stood a girl, as tall as her, shaped like her, with her red hair. She wore a black catsuit and a mask that looked like a cat's face, with cat ears and whiskers.

"Asparagus? Seriously?"

"What," said Thea.

"Asparagus? You like asparagus?"

"What . . . no. You're her. Me. You're me. You need to go home with me. We're supposed to be together." Could she sound any more inane?

The shadow took off her mask. Even though Thea had been expecting it, when she saw her own face she stepped back into the table and almost knocked over the tray of little cakes.

Dr. Patel was farther down the table now, and there was no one behind her in line. She and the shadow were as alone as they could be, in a ballroom.

"I'm not going anywhere with you," said the shadow. Her face was subtly wrong. Thea wondered why, then realized that for the first time she was looking at herself the way other people saw her, not reflected in a mirror. "Why should I? You put me in a box for twelve years! A shadow in a dark box—I barely existed. But here I'm as real as you are. Probably realer—you look sort of faded around the edges. In fact, why don't you stay here and be my shadow? That would be amusing!"

No, it wouldn't. "First of all, I didn't put you in a box for twelve years. My grandmother did. And second of all . . ."

"Well, you didn't take me out, did you? I'm not going anywhere with you, no way, no how. I just wanted to see you in person. When I saw you in the Seeing Ball with Morgan Boringstar, I thought, *I wonder what she's like.* Well let me tell you, I am *not* impressed. Except for the shoes—I do like the shoes, but that's it. And you can tell Morgan that she should find herself another Seeing Ball, because I'm not giving this one back!"

"Well, well, so you've found Thea, Thea!" The satyr Thea had seen dancing with the butterfly woman put his arms around the shadow. She laughed and yanked his long hair, then kissed him loudly on the mouth.

"Come on, Oryx," she said. "Let's go somewhere interesting. This party's lame!"

He laughed and swung her onto the dance floor. As they capered away, over the stream and across the moonlit room, Thea heard, "I saw you talking to her! Did she have my Seeing Ball?"

"No," said Thea. She turned around. Morgan was a little out of breath, still wearing her mask of black feathers. "She said to tell you that she wasn't giving it back."

"That little . . . When I find her, I'm going to put her back in a box. A sewing box—a cigar box—a match box. Let's see how she likes that!"

"I'm sorry, I need to sit down." How faint her voice sounded! Still clutching her plate, Thea turned away from Morgan and walked as steadily as she could to one of the doors, leaning for a moment against the frame, then down a torch-lit hall until she reached a stone arch through which she could see the garden. She stumbled out into the night and sat on one of the benches, putting her plate on her lap.

She could not eat. The nausea was even stronger than before. Was it because she had encountered her shadow? She looked down at the plate and almost cried out in fear. Its porcelain edges were visible through her hands. She held one hand up in front of her. Through it she could see the moonlit garden, with its topiaries black in the moonlight, its trellises on which white flowers bloomed in the darkness. Through her hand she could see the moon and constellations. Why was she fading so quickly? Mrs. Moth has said it would take time, but here in the Other Country, it was taking no time at all.

She had no idea what to do.

A small voice, her own although it sounded suspiciously like Mother Night's, said *You must take care of yourself.* Step one: fish pie. Step two: scalloped potatoes. Step three: asparagus, ugh. But she ate every stalk.

"Finally you're doing something sensible," said Cordelia. The cat was sitting on the bench beside her, yellow eyes shining in the moonlight. "When you're done, I want to lick your plate. I mean the fish part of it."

"Where have you been all day?" asked Thea, finishing the little marzipan cakes. She did not feel better, exactly. But at least she did not feel quite so hollow.

"On cat business, which is Mother Night's business, of course," said the cat. Thea put her plate on the bench, and Cordelia licked the remains of the fish and potatoes.

"I found my shadow, or she found me, but Cordy, it's hopeless." Thea looked down at her ghostly, almost transparent hands. "She blames me for putting her in that box. She doesn't want anything to do with me, unless I become *her* shadow. And everyone says this is something I have to figure out myself—Mother Night won't help me, and I don't know what to do."

"Well," said the cat, licking her paws and washing her face with them, "you can start by thinking like a witch instead of a whiny twelve-year-old. Remember the day you arrived at Miss Lavender's?"

"I'm not that girl anymore," said Thea. That small, scared girl, scarcely larger than the trunk she had lugged through the airport and then onto the train from Boston. She wasn't like that, was she?

"You could have fooled me."

Think like a witch. No, she wasn't that girl anymore. She was a graduate of Miss Lavender's, and even if she didn't know what to do right now, she would figure it out.

Thea took a deep breath. "Cordy, I bet she's still in the castle. She's the part of me that my grandmother cut away, the bad part. Or, you know, rebellious. Angry. She's teasing us now, showing us that she's smarter, better than we are. She likes doing that. So she's still here."

"Then let's go find her," said the cat.

"She stole Raven's cloak of invisibility. I think that's why Morgan hasn't been able to find her all this time. So we need another way to find her. Can you find her by smell?"

"How would I do that?" said Cordelia, looking at her incredulously. "Do you have any idea how big the castle is? I don't think even the castle itself knows! We could look for years."

"I think I know where to start. She's so confident, but it's all on the surface—she doesn't belong here any more than I do. She's lost, just like me. I think she's been hiding in the Library of Lost Books. That's what I would do, hide among the lost things. I think that's why she was toasting marshmallows in the library fireplace. Of course if she looks in the Seeing Ball, she can see us coming, in which case we're out of luck. But she didn't have it earlier—I would have noticed it on her, in that cat outfit. We have to take the chance that she's too occupied or distracted to check. Anyway, this is the only plan I can think of right now. Will you help me?"

"All right," said Cordelia. "I'll even let you carry me, as long as you don't turn me on my back. I'm not a human infant, you know!"

Thea put the cat over her shoulder. She didn't have time to return her plate and cutlery to the ballroom—hopefully someone would find them. "To a witch, any door is every door." Senator Warren had said that, speaking at her graduation. It was probably supposed to be a metaphor, but metaphorical language was poetry, right? And poetry was magic. She walked back to the stone arch that led into the castle. She stood in front of it, clutching Cordelia, and said,

> "Ghosts of thoughts are lying
> on the shelves, rustling
> like a forest of dry leaves.
> Take me to them."

See? Metaphor—or was that a simile? She was getting better at this. Thea stepped through the archway and into the Library of Lost Books.

The library was dark and silent, illuminated only by the moonlight that came through tall, mullioned windows. It gleamed on row upon row of books with gilt lettering on their spines. She put Cordelia down on the floor.

"All right," she said. "Look for someone who smells like me. I mean smell for. You know what I mean."

Cordelia sniffed the air. Thea could see the shining circles of her eyes. Then she turned away and slunk into the darkness. This could take a while . . . but no, just a minute later Cordelia was back.

"Well, that was easy," she said disdainfully. "She may have gotten all the anger, but you got all the brains. They're asleep, right in front of the fireplace."

Thea followed the cat across the dark, cavernous room to a stone fireplace. On a carpet in front of the fireplace, there was . . . nothing. "Invisibility cloak," she said. "Show me where?"

Cordelia nudged the nothing.

Thea knelt down and felt the air . . . yes, it was fabric, scratchy like wool. She pulled it off. There, on the carpet, asleep and smelling distinctly of wine, were her shadow and Oryx the satyr. One of her arms was flung over his hairy chest.

"What now?" asked Cordelia.

"I don't know." She had been doing the next thing and the next, as they occurred to her. Looking down at her shadow, nestled against the satyr, she did not know what to do.

"Well, that's helpful," said the cat in her most disgusted tone. She sat on the stone floor and wrapped her tail around her feet.

Thea sat down beside her cross-legged, set the peacock mask on the floor, and put her chin in her hands. The green dress, black in the moonlight, puddled around her. How do you join a shadow to yourself after it has been snipped away? That was the question.

"If I could get her to back Miss Lavender's, I could ask Miss Gray to rejoin us—or maybe Mrs. Moth would do it? But I don't know how to get her back there without waking her up. And if I wake her, she'll never agree to go with me." The shadow had made that perfectly clear.

"Do you always wait for someone else to solve your problems?" Cordelia asked, as though posing a theoretical question.

Thea put her hands over her eyes, ashamed of herself. Yes, mostly, up to now she had. Her grandmother, and then the teachers at school. But she wasn't in school anymore, was she? She was an adult now, and adults solved their own problems. So did witches.

"Wait." She opened her eyes. Her hands were still in front of her face, but she could see right through them, to the bookshelves across the room. Both of her hands were completely transparent. Quickly, she put them in her lap, where she couldn't see them. She didn't want to know how much she had faded here, so close to her shadow. "Mrs. Moth said something—if only I could remember."

Cordelia yawned, pointedly.

"That's it!" Suddenly, it had come back to her—the conversation over tea, and a chance remark. "Magic is poetry. At least, poetry plus math. I always hated the math part, but all we need is for one plus one to equal one." Carefully, she leaned forward and turned the shadow over—the other Thea made a sound, but did not wake up. Then she sat back and pulled out one of her long red hairs. "You'll have to be both needle and thread," she said to the red strand.

"Thread the needle, sharp as pain,
sew the fabric, strong as grief."

She put the soles of her feet right on the shadow's, her Keds to
the soft black leather boots of the catsuit, and began to sew.

"Join the twain, join them well,
bind them as a single soul,
so they cannot be unbound."

Starting at the heel, up the outside and a few extra stitches at the
toe, down the inside, knot. Then the other foot.

"Sewing spell, join them soundly,
solidly and well."

Once she had knotted the thread again, she stood up. The shadow lay on the floor, just where the moonlight would have cast Thea's
shadow. Thea looked down at her hands. She could no longer see
through them. They were completely solid.

"Well?" said Cordelia.

"I don't know. I think it worked. I remember being at Miss Lavender's and being in the box. If I'd been in that box, I would have
hated me too! I think I do hate me. And my grandmother, and Anne
Featherstone, and my parents for dying, and . . . Cordy, what's wrong
with my face?"

"You're crying. You humans do that."

Thea could feel tears coursing down her cheeks. Suddenly, she
started to sob—loud, heaving sobs that racked her as she leaned forward, hands on her stomach, then fell to her knees. She felt as though
she were going to split apart again, this time from anger and grief.
She had never felt anything so painful—the wracking sobs continued—no, she had, she remembered now. But it had been long ago,
when she was a child. And it all came flooding back—her mother's
soft auburn hair, the sensation of riding on her father's shoulders,
the day she had been told they would not, no never, come back. She
couldn't bear it. She knelt on the cold, hard floor and sobbed.

"You have to get up," said Cordelia. "We have to go home.
Look."

Thea looked up. Through her tears, she saw that it was brighter—
no longer moonlight, but the soft blue light of early morning, beginning to come through the library windows.

"What's wrong with me, Cordy? Why can't I stop crying?"

"You're both of you now." The cat rubbed up against her, a rare
gesture of affection. "Come on. You can do it, you know."

Thea stood up awkwardly and rubbed her hands across her face.
They were slick with tears. She didn't want to ruin the green dress
by wiping them on it, so she just rubbed them against each other,
hoping they would dry. She took a deep breath that hurt her ribs.
Her stomach was still queasy and there was an ache in her chest, but
somehow she felt stronger than before. As though the world had
stopped tilting around her.

"All right, give me a minute."

She knelt beside the satyr and kissed him on one cheek, despite
his bad breath, then stroked his hair. "I liked you—a lot. And honestly, you're pretty hot for someone who's half goat." Then she picked
up the peacock mask from where she had set it down.

"Can we go home now?" Cordelia yawned a wide cat yawn and
blinked her eyes. This time, she seemed genuinely sleepy.

"One more thing. No, two." Thea found the Seeing Ball where
she—the shadow—no, she as the shadow—had left it, behind Volume
VII of *The Collected Poems of Sappho*. It was confusing, having two sets
of memories. Going to school at Miss Lavender's—being in a box for
twelve years, like a long, dreamless sleep—attending her grandmother's funeral—finding herself free in Mother Night's Castle—sitting in
her Boston apartment, watching anime on YouTube and eating take-
out sushi, afraid of everything, college and what the future held for
her—capering around the gardens with Oryx, hiding behind the giant
chess pieces, teasing the fish. Which were her memories? All of them,
she supposed. She felt around the floor next to the satyr—there, the
invisibility cloak, with its scratchy wool. She put it over her arm so that
her hand looked as though it were floating in the air. Then she hoisted
the soft, sleepy cat to her shoulder. Carrying cat and cloak and mask,
she walked to the library door.

> "Morning has come, and morning's star has risen:
> her chamber awaits its radiant messenger.
> Take me there."

She stepped through the library door into Morgan's tower.

The Morningstar was, in fact, not there. Putting Cordelia on the bed, where she promptly curled up and fell asleep, Thea changed into her own clothes. Thank goodness she had brought extra. And Mother Night had said something about chocolate . . . yes, there it was, half a bar in the front pocket of her backpack. She broke off a square and put it into her mouth, chewing it quickly, automatically. But it was the best chocolate she had ever tasted—honestly, ever. Dark, sweet, bitter, creamy . . . had she never actually tasted chocolate before? Oh, for goodness' sake, she was starting to cry again, and her nose was starting to run. Hastily folding the green dress before she could get tears or snot on it, she put it on the bed with the peacock mask on top and the invisibility cloak beside it. Then she took the notebook out of her backpack, tore out a sheet of paper, and left a note, with the Seeing Ball on top to weigh it down:

> *Thank you so much for everything! I got my shadow and sewed it back on—very Peter Pan! Invisibility cloak is to the left <——— If you're on Facebook friend me!!! <3 Thea*

She slung her backpack over one shoulder and draped Cordelia over the other—drat the cat, why couldn't she wake up and walk? She had to keep sniffing so her nose wouldn't drip. Somewhere in her backpack she might have a tissue, but she couldn't search for one while holding Cordelia and trying to come up with a poem. It didn't have to be long, right? Just effective.

> "The greatest magic
> brings you home."

She stepped through the tower door into the kitchen of the headmistress's house.

Mrs. Moth was in an apron making breakfast. "Good morning, Thea," she said. "When we didn't see you yesterday, we figured you'd found your way to the Other Country. Why, look at you!" She said it in the tone of an aunt who has not seen you in a while and remarks on how much you've grown. "Emily, Lavinia," she called. "Thea's back! All of her, thank goodness." Then she held out a paper towel for Thea's dripping nose.

* * *

"Well, how do you feel?" asked Miss Gray. Thea had taken a shower and brushed her teeth, examining herself curiously in the mirror. She looked tired, and her eyes were red, and there was a shadow following her around, everywhere she went. She kept seeing it out of the corner of her eye and flinching. She could not get used to it.

"I don't know." She ate the last spoonful of her oatmeal. "Confused. Sad about my parents. Angry about being put in a box. Glad to be here. Any minute now I'm probably going to burst into tears again. Sometimes I feel like kicking things, and sometimes I feel like dancing around the room. Although I haven't actually done either of those things yet."

"Oh, but you will, my dear," said Miss Lavender. "It's very confusing, being all of yourself. You'll find it quite uncomfortable for a while. But you'll get used to it. We all do."

"Coffee, anyone?" asked Mrs. Moth.

"Not for me," said Thea. "I think I'll go to Booktopia for a latte. There was a book on writing I wanted to get—John Gardner." Maybe even the Anne Lamott.

"Good for you," said Miss Gray. "I always liked your pieces in *The Broomstick*, especially that article on Hans Christian Andersen. He really was a charming man, although terribly insecure."

"And Sam's quite attractive," said Mrs. Moth. "Though very young."

"This is about *literature*, not romance," said Miss Gray. "Anyway, you think anyone under a century is young. Have a good time, Thea."

"I'll try," said Thea. Miss Gray had read something of hers and actually liked it! Maybe she could write some poems, or an article. That shouldn't be too hard, right? The novels could come later . . . She smiled at herself, then sniffed again and wiped her nose with the balled-up paper towel.

On the way out, she scratched Cordelia behind the ears. The cat curled up more tightly on the parlor sofa, purring in her sleep. Thea put on her jacket and scarf, then stepped into the cold New England morning, her shadow accompanying her up the path and into the town, toward the bookstore and anywhere else she might want to go.

The Sensitive Woman

There are days on which I am a thunderstorm,
and days on which I am an eggshell. Today,
I am so fragile that if you breathed on me,
I would break apart. The pieces of me would lie
on the kitchen floor, over the hard gray tiles,
my torso in fragments, my heart like a shattered cup,
one eye near the sink, one near the refrigerator,
staring upward, blinking.

There is a story about a woman so sensitive
that she could be bruised by the brush of a swallow's wing,
that the cold light of the moon would burn her cheek.
There is a story about a woman who wept at the fall
of a rose petal, at the sight of a spider's web,
at a line from Keats's "Ode to a Nightingale."
There is a story about a woman who could not be
consoled when she heard a single measure of Brahms,
or watched the sun setting over Budapest.
Her tears flowed into the Danube.
There are days on which I am all these women.

I would like to write a poem comparing myself
to a thunderstorm raging down the valleys,
battering the rocks, flattening the willow trees.
But today a raindrop could drown me. Today, a breeze
could tear me apart, send ragged bits of me flying
like white tufts of milkweed from the pod.
Hush. Don't breathe, don't speak, handle me gently.
Today, a word of yours, no matter how kind,
would be too hard to bear.

The Bear's Wife

I went to the bear's house
reluctantly: my father would have a pension
for his old age, my mother a pantry filled
with food for winter. My brothers would go to school,
my little sister—all she wanted, she said,
was a dolly of her very own. I went
dutifully. Like a good daughter.

In the bear's house there were carpets with dim, rich colors
from Isfahan, and mahogany furniture,
and brocade curtains. More bedrooms than I could count,
a ballroom in which I was the only dancer,
a library filled with books. And electric lights!
But I chose a candle to see him by—the bear,
my husband. The wax dripped.

He woke, reproaching me, and it was gone—
house, carpets, furniture, curtains, books,
even the emptiness of empty rooms.
I was alone in the forest.

If I returned to my father's house, they would greet me
with cakes and wine. My mother would draw me aside.
This is what comes of marrying a bear, she would say,
but now it's over. You can live a normal life,
marry again, have children that are not bears,
become a respectable woman.

There was the path back to my father's house.
Instead I turned toward the pathless forest,

knowing already what the choice entailed:
walking up glass mountains in iron shoes,
riding winds to the corners of the earth,
answering ogres' riddles. And at the end
the bear, my husband, whom I barely knew.
And yet, I walked into the dangerous trees,
knowing it was my life, knowing I chose it
over safety, maybe over sanity. Because it was mine,
because it was life.

The Bear's Daughter

She dreams of the south. Wandering through the silent castle,
where snow has covered the parapets and the windows
are covered with frost, like panes of isinglass,
she dreams of pomegranates and olive trees.

But to be the bear's daughter is to be a daughter, as well,
of the north. To have forgotten a time before
the tips of her fingers were blue, before her veins
were blue like rivers flowing through fields of ice.

To have forgotten a time before her boots
were elk-leather lined with ermine.

Somewhere in the silent castle, her mother is sleeping
in the bear's embrace, and breathing pomegranates
into his fur. She is a daughter of the south,
with hair like honey and skin like orange-flowers.

She is a nightingale's song in the olive groves.

And her daughter, wandering through the empty garden,
where the branches of yew trees rubbing against each other
sound like broken violins,

dreams of the south while a cold wind sways the privet,
takes off her gloves, which are lined with ermine, and places
her hands on the rim of the fountain, in which the sun
has scattered its colors, like roses trapped in ice.

A Country Called Winter

In winter, the snow comes down as softly as feathers. I have always loved to watch it. It's different, of course, once it's fallen: thick, heavy, difficult to walk through. In Boston, the snow plows come out almost as soon as the first flakes land on the sidewalk. They make narrow paths, and the snow piles up on either side, so when you walk to class, it's between two mountain ridges, like a miniature Switzerland.

That's how Kay described it to me one morning, while we were sitting in my dorm room, drinking Swiss Miss hot chocolate that I had heated up in the microwave I wasn't supposed to have. He had the most charming accent that sounded, to my ear, sort of German and sort of French, and that look foreign students have. They are generally better groomed, their clothes are better proportioned, and they have the latest electronics. They listen to avant garde music and talk about art. Of course that's partly because they are the children of diplomats and businessmen—the ones who can make the choice to come to an expensive American university. Kay was the son of the Danish ambassador, but he had lived in so many countries that when I asked him where he was from, he simply said, "I am European." Once, he even took me to the art museum on a date. Catch an American student doing that!

He was an undergraduate, and I had just started my M.A. I was a little uncomfortable about that. He was only two years younger than me, but at the university, the undergraduate/graduate divide seemed almost unsurmountable. And anyway, I wasn't looking for a boyfriend. I wanted to finish my M.A. year with a high enough grade point average to go directly into the Ph.D. program. All I was planning to think about that year were my classes in American literature: *The Poetry of Emily Dickinson*, *Emerson and the Transcendentalists*, *The Novel from World War I to Postmodernism*, and *The*

Immigrant Experience, which I was not particularly excited about. I'd lived my own immigrant experience, and didn't want to read about anyone else's.

When I was a little girl, I asked my mother why she had come to the United States, with one suitcase and an infant daughter, leaving behind her parents, her language, everything she had ever known.

"We come from a cold country," she had told me. "Do you know, Vera, in that country the king lives in a palace built of white stone with veins of quartz that resemble ice. The streets are made of ice between snow banks, and there are no automobiles—only sleighs. They used to be pulled by reindeer, but nowadays they are electronic."

Vera was not my real name, but my English name, which she had given me when we landed at Logan airport. It sounded like part of my name in our native language, which I will transliterate Veriska, although Americans have difficulty pronouncing it properly. In our language, it means Snow Flower.

I would write it here in our alphabet, but the letters aren't on my computer. My Apple Mackintosh does not yet speak the language of snow.

I was six years old, just about to start first grade, when we came to America. I was put in an English immersion program. The school administration had no choice, really. There was no one in the school, or even the school district, who spoke our language. We come from a small country, with a difficult language—agglutinative, and not related to any Indo-European tongue. The alphabet resembles a series of curlicues, like frost on a windowpane. If you're not familiar with it, you won't know where one letter begins and another ends. Some of the letters are not letters at all, but ideas, or more properly, modes of thinking. There is a letter, for example, that stands for memory. If you put it at the beginning of a word, it means something has been remembered. Or, if you add the letter for negation, that something has been forgotten.

Even the name of our country is difficult to pronounce for English speakers. Instead of spelling it out phonetically, we refer to it by its name in translation: Winter.

There was a small community of my countrymen and women in Boston, all my mother's age or older. Many of them had fled after the most recent revolution. The history of my country in the twentieth century is a series of revolutions and conquests. I asked my mother who would want to conquer the country she described to me: a series of valleys between high mountains, where in summer the snow might melt for several months in the lower valleys, to be replaced by small white flowers that resembled snow, and winter seemed to last forever. Even in June the blossoming fruit trees might be covered with a layer of ice. The cold made our small, hard apples sweeter, tastier, than they were anywhere else. Cabbages and turnips were staples. Most crops were grown in large greenhouses that protected tender plants from the cold.

Countries in the lower valleys, my mother answered. Before the Second World War, in warmer regions, our primary export had been a valued commodity. In the days before electric refrigeration, everyone wanted ice. Now, of course, there was tourism: skiers and snowboarders valued our steep slopes, and mountain climbers came to conquer the high peaks of our mountains.

Because I could not speak English that first year, I could not make friends. It was a lonely year for me.

Eventually I learned English, but I never quite learned how to be an American child. Perhaps I had come here too late. Or perhaps it was something in me that caused me to turn inward rather than toward other children, and I would have been the same even in my native Winter, never quite fitting in there either. I found my refuge in books, particularly books about this new country I could barely understand. *Little House on the Prairie* seemed to me the most wonderful fairy tale about the great wide west. Jo, Beth, Meg, and Amy March were four princesses growing up in a magical place called Concord, Massachusetts—just close enough to be real and yet far enough away to seem like a land lost in mists. I was in love with Tom Sawyer, and bitterly jealous of Becky Thatcher, for whom he walked on top of a fence. No one had walked on top of a fence for me. I liked those stories better than the stories in the old book from our country that my mother read to me, in which women married white bears and then had to travel to the ends of the earth, climbing mountains of ice in iron shoes, to rescue their bear husbands from frost giants. Why marry a bear in the first place? I wondered. Why not go to a one-room schoolhouse, form settlements, write for magazines as Jo was doing? Tom Sawyer was a trickster, like the fox in our fairy tales, whose pelt was as white as snow. He would sneak into your house and steal your fire, like a ghost. Huck Finn was like one of the ice trolls—uncivilized and uncouth, but somehow fascinating.

Although my mother read me these fairy tales, she did not like to discuss the history of our country. "We have left all that behind," she said. But the woman she hired to stay with me after school while she worked at Boston University as a research librarian told me about the two princes who had founded our country, climbing high in the mountains to establish their territory above the Roman legions who were harrying them below. They had married the daughters of the king of the ice trolls—tall, beautiful women whose eyes were the color of rocks. Their descendants had battled each other a thousand years for the throne. She had taken the American name Anna, and I called her Nana Anna. It was she who helped me retain my native tongue, for my mother rarely spoke in our language. "Why should I?" she said. "We are never going back, and it makes me sad."

When I was in high school, Nana Anna finally succumbed to lung cancer from the small brown cigarettes she was incessantly smoking, hand-rolled from a tobacco flavored with vanilla. After school—I had been admitted to Boston Latin Academy, one of the prestigious public schools that require an examination—I would go to her small apartment in Alston, and eventually her hospital room in Massachusetts General Hospital, to sit with her for hours, doing my homework. One day in the hospital, she motioned me to approach her bed. Closer, closer, she motioned, impatiently. With her small, frail, claw-like hand, she pulled me down by the lapel of my school jacket and whispered, in a voice that was almost gone, the ghost of a voice, "Versika, when it is time, you must go back."

I did not know what she meant, and did not want to distress her by asking. Anyway, I was American now—the previous year, my mother and I had become citizens. I had no desire to go back to Winter. I did not think of it as my native country anymore—did not even remember what it looked like, except in dreams that were probably based on my mother's stories of frost giants and streets paved with ice and quince trees grown in glass houses. I spoke my native language adequately but not well, and rarely practiced it anymore now that Nana Anna was so sick. Somewhere along the way, I had decided to become as American as possible. I wore blue jeans and had a tattoo of falling snowflakes on my left wrist that scandalized my mother, because well-behaved girls did not get tattoos. I read Sylvia Plath.

My mother wanted me to study library science, "Because you like books so much, Vera," she said, "and it's a practical profession." But I told her I wanted to study literature.

"Well, perhaps you can become a teacher," she replied.

There were only a few people at Nana Anna's funeral—three old men and one young woman who said she was a distant relative. One of the old men came up to my mother and bowed, then spoke with her too rapidly for me to understand what he was saying. But among the words, I recognized one that meant "princess"—literally, "king's daughter." When I asked my mother about it, she said, "Anna was a member of the royal court, a descendant of one of the two families that have, for time out of mind, fought over Winter's throne. In our country, she was lady-in-waiting to the queen. It was her hereditary right."

How strange that this old woman who had taken care of me had been a member of the royal family! Remembering her one-bedroom apartment with its tiny kitchen, I felt sorry for her. She had been meant for palaces made of white stone with veins of quartz.

But I had the SAT to study for. I could not spent too much time thinking about the history of Winter—about which, anyway, I knew only the fragments Nana Anna had told me.

There were boyfriends here and there, in those years—a couple of casual ones in high school and a steady one in college, at Amherst, where I had gotten a full ride—half scholarships, half grants. I even thought we might become engaged, until the day he told me he was in love with a girl I thought was my best friend. Several months later, when he broke up with her and told me that I was the one, had always been the one—that he had just needed to make sure—I had already been admitted to a graduate program. Sorry, I told him. I really don't have time for a relationship right now.

I was right—the M.A. program took all the time and energy I had, that and being an R.A. in an undergraduate dorm. At least it gave me a place to live so I didn't have to stay at home with my mother. I could never have afforded my own apartment in Boston. I settled down to write my semester papers, determined to do as well as I could. That would be my life, I figured—classes during the day, evenings doing research in Mugar Library.

And then I met Kay.

I have always preferred winter, probably because I was born in Winter, in February, when my mother tells me the capital city was encased in ice and the doctor had to come by electric sleigh through a snowstorm. I love to see the first leaves change, love to feel the cold breath of autumn coming. Seasonal allergies have something to do with it. June and July, I live on Claritin. The pollen from all the blossoming trees gives me a terrible headache. But after September comes, it seems as though the air regains a crystalline quality. It feels like clear water, like something hard and soft at the same time—feathers that can cut. Then the leaves turn and fall, like a splendid sunset lying on the sidewalks, and the first snows come, white and fresh, as though the earth is putting on her wedding gown.

Christmas has always been my favorite holiday. In my country, gifts are not brought by Santa Claus. The Lady in the Moon herself comes down from the sky in her silver sleigh, drawn by snow geese that have put on their white plumage for winter. Next to her sits the white fox who eats the moon each month before the Lady renews it again. With the help of all the stars, who look like elves in sparkling tights and dresses, she distributes gifts to children throughout the land. Although my mother had given up many of our native customs, each year she decorated the tree with a moon on top, papier-mâché stars hanging from the branches, felt reindeer, and gingerbread men. We would leave out elderberry wine for the Lady in the Moon and a plate of oat cakes with a wedge of cheese for the geese and fox. The next morning, the oat cakes always had small bites taken out of it, and the cheese was eaten into a crescent shape.

I met Kay during the first snowfall. He bumped into me as I was walking to class, thinking about my paper on the rhetoric of mourning in the poetry of Emily Dickinson. I slipped and fell on the icy sidewalk. "*Undskyld!*" he said, then switched to English. "I'm sorry, how stupid of me—I should have watched where I was going. Let me help you." He took off his right glove and reached down a pale, firm hand. I recognized him from my class on the Transcendentalists, which was a 500-level course for both upper-class undergrads and M.A. students. He was the one who always did the reading and talked about the Transcendentalists as though their ideas mattered for more than the final exam. I had noticed him—he was, after all, tall and blond and very good-looking. He was hard not to notice. But I had thought of him as simply another undergrad.

What made him so much more exciting than other boys I had dated? Well, he was European—more sophisticated, more intellectual. He could talk about postmodern literary theory, although after several beers his utterances became as convoluted as Lacan's. His area was modern European literature. He had been taking courses in the American Studies department simply for a distribution requirement. But he could also be moody, go silent for days at a time, sitting on his dorm room window seat and looking out at the snow. I asked him once if all that theory was good for him.

Still, there was something in me that was attracted to him. His family came from a small village in Denmark beside a glacier, where the primary industry was the ski season. Sometimes he seemed like a breath of cold mountain air. We had been dating for several months and our relationship was going well—he was going to stay in Boston for Christmas, and I had already told him that he could come celebrate with me and my mother—when Gerda showed up.

It was after Thanksgiving Break. We were sitting in our Transcendentalism class, waiting for Professor Feldman (Bob to those of us who were graduate students, but only in office hours and at departmental cocktail parties) to show up when in walked a girl—well, a woman, but she was not much older than me. She was wearing a pair of red boots that came up over her knees, and her black hair was cut in a Louise Brooks bob. She stood in front of the class and said, "Hi everyone. I have some bad news—Professor Feldman had a heart attack over the break. We don't know yet when he'll be able to come back to class. I was his TA last semester, so I'm going to fill in for him. I'm a grad student, so don't bother calling me professor. You can just call me Gerda. All right, let's see who did the reading. Pop quiz!"

She was in my department, but I hadn't met her—she had passed her oral exam over the summer and was already working on her dissertation. After the class I introduced myself. "Oh, right, Vera," she said. "You and the other M.A. students don't need to take the final exam. Just turn in a 20-page paper on the last day of class. Have you written a prospectus already? No? Well, how about turning it in next Friday?"

Later, Kay told me that she had "Robber Girl" tattooed across her shoulder blades, right where you could see it if she wore a low-cut dress, or maybe a bathing suit. It was the name of her rock band. Yes, she had a rock band with a couple of students from the Berklee College of Music—she was the lead singer and played guitar. They toured during the summer months, doing covers of the Eurythmics and other 80s groups. I wondered how he knew—when had he seen her bare back? But it was the sort of information Gerda volunteered freely. Perhaps she had simply told him during office hours.

That was after the semester was over, of course—after we had picked up our final papers from her box in the department mail room. I was relieved to have gotten an A on the paper and for the semester. Gerda was much too smart to mess around with the university's sexual harassment policy. No, she just stood in front of the class in her high red boots, wearing skinny jeans or a short denim skirt and a black turtleneck, talking about feminism and sexuality in Emily Dickinson's poems, which was the topic of her doctoral dissertation. "If Dickinson could have fucked death, she would have," Gerda said once, clearly not caring what anyone said on her course evaluations.

She was a good teacher, I'll give her that. She found meanings in Dickinson's poems that I had not seen. I had admired them for their artistic and intellectual engagement. Gerda revealed their incandescence. Kay always paid particular attention in that class, but then he had paid attention to Professor Feldman as well. It was only later that I realized there was more to it than caring about Dickinson's subtext.

Just before Christmas, he told me that we should take a break, that he had to focus on exams and didn't have time for a relationship. There was no celebration with my mother after all—he insisted that he had to study. By the time I came back to campus in January, he and Gerda were dating.

When I found out from my friend Stephanie, who was a work-study receptionist in the main office and knew all the departmental gossip, I spent a week crying myself to sleep at night, sobbing into my pillow. But Kay didn't know that. I didn't bother asking him for an explanation, and recriminations have never been my style. I have always prided myself on my ability to let things go. After all,

I've had plenty of practice. When I was a little girl, I let go of an entire country.

One day, we ran into each other at the new café that had opened at the edge of campus, on Commonwealth Avenue. Blue Moon, it was called—organic, fair trade, locally sourced. There were scones with chia seeds in them, scones with açai berries. Smoothies that combined mango and kale.

"Vera," he said. "I've been meaning to text you—"

"I already know," I said. "About you and Gerda."

"I really like you," he said, as though it were an apology. "Like, really like. But Gerda, I don't know. We're just on the same wavelength."

But Gerda. I suppose at some level, I had known from the moment she walked in with her high red boots. I had simply not wanted to see that he was drifting away from me like snow. Even when she was standing at the front of the class and he was the undergrad challenging her phallic interpretation of Emily Dickinson's "A narrow fellow in the grass"—"Sometimes a snake is just a snake," he would say—there was something between them, a solidarity. You could tell that despite their differences, they lived in the same intellectual and emotional time zone. They synched.

"I hope you're happy with her," I said. "I'm sure she'll be happy with you." Why wouldn't she be? Any disagreements would be smoothed over by his blue Danish eyes, the perfection of his cheekbones.

Christmas was strange that year. Men and women I did not know came to the apartment and talked to my mother in the walk-in closet she used as a sewing room. They spoke in the language of Winter, but so low and rapidly that I could not hear them through the keyhole, although I tried. I particularly wondered about one woman dressed in a long white coat with silver embroidery all over it, wearing a white fur hat.

"Who was that?" I asked my mother.

"That was the Matriarch of the Orthodox Church," she replied. "Her Holiness is the highest religious authority in our country."

"What is she doing here?" I asked. I had heard of the Holy Mother, but only in Nana Anna's stories. Somehow, she had not seemed real to me, any more than the palace made of white stone or the glass houses with their orchards of flowering trees. But this priestess of the Lady Moon was real the way dreams are real—improbable, and yet indisputably sitting in our small living room, drinking my mother's espresso.

"Paying her respects," said my mother. "Vera, I smell something burning. Did you seal the jam pockets properly?"

Of course not. I never sealed the jam pockets properly. My mother always sealed their edges so the jam did not run out into the pan, but somehow I never managed to. The jam always ran out, overflowed the sides of the pan, and dripped down onto the electric burners. My baking was always accompanied by the smell of burnt sugar.

Winter is a cold country. Most of our deserts incorporate jam, dried fruit, or candied nuts—ingredients that can be stored almost indefinitely during the long, cold months. They are made of hearty grains—barley, oats, rye. Into them we mix cinnamon, nutmeg, ginger.

I rushed into the kitchen to rescue the jam pockets, and by the time I came out again, the Matriarch was gone.

But it was more than a matter of strange visitors coming at all hours. My mother seemed agitated, distracted. When I asked her what was wrong, she said only, "I'm getting old," which was patently untrue. Her black hair was touched with gray, and she had lines of laughter and worry around her eyes, but she was as beautiful as ever—still the woman in the only photograph I had of her with my father, at their wedding. She was wearing an elaborate wedding gown, he was in his military uniform.

"What was his rank?" I asked her when I was in high school. I was curious about this man with the fierce mustache, who had died when I was only a child.

"I do not remember," she had answered. It was more likely that she did not want to remember. All I knew was that he had died in one of our innumerable revolutions, defending the king—Nana Anna had told me that.

To be honest, I was glad when Christmas break was over and I could go back to school. At least I could replace worrying about my mother with working on my papers and avoiding Kay. I transferred out of *Elegance and Anxiety: The Age of Wharton and James* when Stephanie told me he was registered for the course.

* * *

A nd then spring failed to come. In April, the snow did not melt. The forecasters shrugged as though to say, sometimes that happens in Massachusetts. But in May it did not melt either. The temperature did not get above thirty-two degrees Fahrenheit. When June came and the temperature still hovered around freezing, the Weather Channel started talking about freak cold snaps, global cooling, a new ice age.

By that time, I assumed Kay had gone back to Denmark for the summer break. Of course I was still on campus, studying for my oral exam and R.A.ing for the high school juniors and seniors taking summer courses, trying out college for the first time. Anyway, I lived in Boston—I had nowhere else to go.

But one day, I got a text on my cell phone: *V need to talk to you please K.*

Why? I texted back.

To talk about us.

Well, that wasn't exactly an answer, was it?

What about?

Please??? I'll buy coffee. Blue Moon @ 2?

Fine. What was I going to do, refuse to see him altogether? That would just prove to him that I cared, and I didn't. Well, I did, but I didn't want him to know that. Anyway, it was uncivilized. Only high school girls who had watched too much reality TV behaved like that.

He was waiting for me at a table near the front of the café, with a small cappuccino topped with cinnamon, my favorite. He still had perfect cheekbones, but just above his right cheekbone, at the corner of his eye, was a rectangular bandaid. Had he cut himself shaving? No, it was too high for a shaving cut. Well, I would not ask him about it. I was no longer his girlfriend, after all. Let Gerda do that.

"All right, what is it?" I asked, sitting down. He slid the cappuccino over to me.

"I know I messed up," he said. "I should have told you about Gerda. I'm really sorry—really really sorry. Is there any way we can start over?"

I looked at him, astonished. "Start over like . . . what? Like it never happened? What about Gerda, anyway? Where is she? And what are you doing here? Shouldn't you be in Denmark?"

"That's over," he said. "I broke it off with her. She was—well, she was kind of nuts, and also kind of cruel. It's as though she kept sticking this knife into me—metaphorically, I mean. With the things she would say, telling me loved me, and then that she didn't want to see me anymore, then calling me the next day and telling me to come over. It's like she wanted to punish me for caring about her. And she was so negative—she would laugh at me for things like my mom sending me cookies from home—I mean the embassy, not home home. She called me sentimental. I don't know where she is now—she said she was going on tour with Robber Girl, and then she just left. The last I heard from her, she was in Austin, Texas. She hasn't texted me since. But honestly, I don't care where she is. Come on, I know I messed up, but I care about you more than I've ever cared about anyone. Please, can we start over?"

I sipped my cappuccino. I didn't know what to say. On the one hand, he had behaved like a complete asshole. On the other hand, he had very blue eyes, with long lashes. He looked at me pleadingly. That bandaid was incongruous on his perfect face.

"I have to think about it," I finally said, putting my coffee cup down and pushing back my chair. I tried to be nonchalant, but I almost tipped it over as I stood up.

"Sure," he said. "I get it, I really do. Take as long as you need to. Like, a week? I'll text you in a week."

"Thanks for the coffee," I said. "I'm going now."

"You'll let me know in a week, right?" he said, looking up at me anxiously. "I think I was scared of how I felt about you. I think that's why I messed up with Gerda."

"A week," I said, making no promises. But I could already feel myself weakening. He looked at me so appealingly, after all, like a child who wanted approval. Would it be so hard to care about him again? Had I ever actually stopped?

I texted Stephanie, to catch up on the departmental gossip. *What happened between Gerda and Kay?*

It only took her a moment to respond. *I heard they had a big fight. He broke up with her, she threw her Norton Anthology of American Literature at him, and it hit a mirror in his dorm room. He got some glass close to his eye. Had to go to the emergency room to get it out plus a couple of stitches. That girl is batshit crazy.*

Why hadn't he told me about that? Probably because he was ashamed of it, of having gotten involved with someone who would pull a stunt like that. And also of being hurt by a girl.

When I don't know what to do about a situation, I ask my mother. Kay was a situation I didn't know what to do about, so I went home.

I sent my mother a text to let her know I was coming, but she didn't answer. Well, she often had her notifications off—if she turned them off by accident, she never knew how to turn them back on again. She was hopeless at technology. It had taken me a year to convince her to give up her flip-phone for something more practical. It was Thursday, which was her weekday off, so she wouldn't be at the library.

"Mom!" I called as I pushed open the front door. "Mom, are you home?"

No answer, but I heard the murmur of voices from the living room. Did she have guests?

I walked from the hall into the living room. My mother was standing by the fireplace that had once been functional in our nineteenth-century brownstone, but was now purely decorative. Around her stood a group of men and women in business suits, with sashes arranged diagonally across their chests. I recognized the light blue and white of Winter's national flag. There was the Matriarch, in her white hat. On either side of her stood a priestess in a white robe with silver collar and cuffs. But most prominent among them was a woman in a red dress, the color of geraniums. In that company, my mother looked plain and small in her black t-shirt and jeans.

"Vera!" she said, as though startled to see me.

The woman in the red dress turned sharply toward me, then looked me up and down.

"Your Royal Highness," she said. She was tall and striking, with short white hair and a sharp nose. I was startled when she made me a deep curtsey. The men and women in sashes bowed or curtseyed, according to whether they were wearing trousers or skirts. The Matriarch and her priestesses remained upright.

"Excuse me?" I said. "I don't understand . . ."

"Vera," said my mother, coming forward. Suddenly, she was the most authoritative person in that room. The transformation took me by surprise—my mother did not often take charge, except in the library. "This is Baroness Hapsenkopf"—at least, that is the closest approximation in English. "She is the prime minister of Winter. When you were a little girl and your father was killed by his younger brother, she helped us escape, or we would surely have been imprisoned by him and his allies. He was not a good ruler—under his management, the country took on a great deal of debt to finance industries that have not made a profit. Now there is inflation, and no money left to repair the roads or educate the children. There is discontent among the people. Three months ago, he was overthrown by the army. The loyaltists who helped your father were released from prison, and they have been attempting to form a new government under the Baroness. Now, they would like you, as the only direct descendant in the royal line, to return as ruler."

"But my father—" I said.

"Was Luthorion VII, King of Winter," said Baroness Hapsenkopf. "You will be Veriska II. The first Veriska was a warrior queen who battled against the Ice Trolls. What we need now is not a warrior but an economist, a ruler who can repair roads, fund schools, and create jobs for the people. And the Ice Trolls have long been our allies. I have been approached by the Ice King himself, who has offered his son in marriage to cement an alliance between our nations. You are, of course, under no obligation to accept, but it would be an advantageous match."

For a moment, I could not think of anything to say. It was as though the entire world had suddenly shifted under me, as though reality was not at all what I had thought, but something else altogether. The Baroness and the semi-circle of dignitaries from Winter were staring at me, as was my mother—waiting. I had to say something. But what?

"I'm neither a warrior nor an economist," I said, finally. "I'm not qualified to be queen of anything. I mean, I'm just a grad student. The most responsibility I've ever had is being an R.A." This was ridiculous—I had an oral exam to study for, and suddenly I was supposed to rule Winter? Marry an Ice Troll? Fix an economy when I could barely keep track of my credit card balance, even with the banking app? And yet suddenly, a great many things in my life that had perplexed me came into focus, as though I had put on a pair of glasses for the first time. All the pieces of a complicated puzzle were fitting together. They showed me a picture: of Winter, and who my father had been, and why my mother claimed to have forgotten his rank. No wonder Nana Anna had taken such care to teach me the history of my country. A moment ago, the future had stretched before me, shapeless, formless. Now, it took a definite shape, as though flakes of snow had fallen and formed a pattern: a woman made of snow.

"Veriska," said my mother, calling me by my full name for the first time since I was a child. "Your choice has repercussions here as well. You see, the snow has not gone away. It is still cold in Boston. Winter is more than a country—it is also an idea. It exists among the mountains, and also in the imagination. There must be a king or queen of Winter to maintain balance among the seasons."

Okay, I sort of got that. I had been trained to understand metaphors. I mean, it didn't really make sense, but then neither did a lot of other things that were nevertheless real and tangible. Somewhere, there was probably a Summer kingdom as well. But I was still not comfortable with the whole concept. "Why does it have to be a king or queen?" I asked. "Can't you elect a president or something?"

"You may abdicate, if you wish," said the Matriarch in her sonorous voice. "But doing so will plunge our country once again into chaos. There is no other clear heir to the throne, and several claimants in an indirect line who will fight each other to death if given the opportunity."

So a constitutional monarchy it was, then. A republic was clearly not in the cards. "Can I have some time to think?" I asked.

"Of course," replied the Matriarch. She looked at her wristwatch. "We can give you an hour."

One hour to make the most important decision of my life? These people were crazy, the whole situation was crazy. I was about to say that when I saw the Baroness's face. It was carefully neural, but there were dark circles under her eyes and cheekbones.

Nana Anna had told me about the men and women who had been sent to prison—or worse, to labor camps in the mountains— for supporting the last king. She had simply neglected to mention that he was my father. The dignitaries in front of me, with their blue and white sashes, were some of those people.

"All right, one hour," I said. I walked out of the apartment and down to our street of brownstones, then turned and made my way to Commonwealth Avenue. It was the middle of summer, but the people who passed me were still wearing winter coats. I walked around for a while, randomly, then went down to the Charles River and stared at the ice still floating on the surface. It wasn't thick enough to walk on—there was black water underneath. Should I agree to become Winter's queen? I felt completely inadequate to the task.

Suddenly, the ice on the river cracked into large chunks. The chunks had nowhere to go, so they simply lay on top of the water. The cracks made a pattern in the language of Winter: they spelled out *Queen Veriska*. I rubbed my eyes, absolutely certain that I was hallucinating.

"It's not an illusion." Who had said that, in the language of my country?

Next to me stood a woman in a light blue dress, with a white fur collar and cuffs. She was wearing a white fur hat on her gray hair and carrying what I thought was a ruff of the same fur until I realized it was a fox as white as snow. Behind her stood a sleigh carved of white wood with silver runners, to which were harnessed six white geese.

"Lady Moon," I said. I mean, it was obvious who she was— Nana Ana had told me enough stories. Either I was ready to be committed to a mental hospital, or I was having an encounter with a supernatural being.

"Winter needs you," she said. "You see, it is calling to you all the way here in Boston."

"But I don't know how to be a queen." I looked back down at the ice. Now it was spelling out *Come home Queen Veriska*.

"When have you known how to do anything before you did it?" she asked. "Did you know how to swim before you learned at Walden Pond in summer camp? Did you know how to write a paper before your eleventh grade teacher taught you in Honors English? You will learn this as well. Baroness Hapsenkopf will teach you, as will your mother, the Queen Dowager."

It was disconcerting how much Lady Moon knew about me. But then, she was Winter's equivalent to Santa Claus. She probably knew everything.

"This is different," I said. "No one was going to drown if I didn't learn to swim but me. No one else was going to get an F on her paper if I failed. But if I fail as queen . . . Anyway, I don't understand this whole business about balancing the seasons."

"The Snow King or Queen brings winter," she said. "Then as the year turns, the King or Queen of Summer—currently Rudolph IV—brings back warmth and sunlight, banishing the cold and darkness until it is time for winter again. But the two monarchs must coordinate carefully. If Rudi comes while snow is still lying on the ground, it will cause terrible floods. So you must work with him, you must hand off responsibilities, as it were—he has been waiting for months now for the coronation of Winter's queen." I could tell from the tone of her voice that she was being patient, but I had maybe five or ten more minutes of her putting up with my nonsense. At least, that's the way Nana Anna would have said it.

It all sounded—well, a little crazy, and like a lot of responsibility. How in the world was I supposed to do all this?

"Hold out your hand," she said. "Over the ice. Just there—hold it steadily." I had overestimated: by her tone, I had maybe a minute more of her patience. I didn't think she would frown at me the way Nana Anna had. She was much more likely to turn me into a rock, as she had the daughter of Ivor the Ice Troll in fairy tales, and then smash me to smithereens.

I held my hand over the icy river. What was this supposed to do?

The cracks in the ice reformed themselves into the words *What do you wish, O Queen?*

What did I wish? I didn't even know anymore. "I wish winter would end," I said. I did, at least, want that. Let the high school students play Ultimate Frisbee on the university's small patches of green space. Let people eat ice cream while walking down the street in T-shirts.

Your wish is our command, wrote the ice, and then it broke along those cracks. The pieces of ice stood up on end and danced on the choppy black water, then melted. The sun came out from behind the gray clouds. It was not warm, exactly—it was still a winter sun. But it was something.

"I shall tell Rudi that you are on your way," said Lady Moon with a tight-lipped smile, the same smile her fox seemed to have on his face. I could tell that I had sorely tried her patience. "Run along, Veriska. Give Queen Agata my best wishes, and tell the Matriarch that I will be back in Winter for Christmas, as usual."

I walked back to the apartment in a daze. When I entered the living room again, I walked up to Baroness Hapsenkopf and said,

"All right, I'll do it. I'll be Veriska II. I mean, you'll have to teach me how, but I'll try."

"What convinced you?" asked the Matriarch, sounding as though she did not particularly approve of me—but I was the only Veriska II she had, so she would have to make the best of it.

"Lady Moon," I said. "She . . . well, we had a talk. I mean, she did most of the talking."

My mother looked at me with astonishment, but the Matriarch nodded as though she were not at all surprised.

"Then it is time to leave," said the Baroness. "There is a helicopter waiting for us on the roof."

Somehow, I had been expecting a sleigh drawn by snow geese, or something equally improbable. But a helicopter would work as well. I turned to go pack, but no, I would not need to pack. There was nothing here I needed, not even my tattered and heavily underlined copy of *The Complete Poems of Emily Dickinson*, and anyway from now on my packing would be done for me. I had more important things to do—a country to save, a balance to restore, if I could just learn how.

"All right," I said. "I'm ready."

A week later, I got a text on my cell phone. It was still my old iPhone with an international plan. I was getting 3G even in Winter.

Holy crap it's all over the Daily Free Press you're like a queen. Do I call you majesty or what. Summer finally here.

I was standing in the greenhouse attached to the palace, under the quince trees. I had spent the morning in a meeting with the finance minister, and would spend the afternoon in a meeting with the ambassadors of Sweden, Norway, and Denmark. Should I write back? At least to tell Kay that I was meeting with a representative of his country. Or not—I doubt he was texting me to hear about politics. Why was he texting me? Oh yeah, it was a week after our meeting in the Blue Moon café.

Winter here. In royal palace. Coronation yesterday, so yes, I'm officially queen. Your majesty, ma'am, whatever. ;)

The response came almost as soon as I had written mine.

So no hope of getting back together I guess. Ma'am.

I had to laugh. The gall of him! I still cared about him—I did, didn't I? Despite the whole Gerda incident. But at a royal reception, I had met the crown prince of Trollheim, whose name was Edrik. Trolls are a lot better looking than you would expect. He had really pretty blue eyes, and excellent taste in British rock bands. We had a long discussion of existentialism once we'd escaped from the reception with a handful of canapés. I didn't know if I wanted to marry him, but I wasn't ruling out the possibility. He wasn't sure how he felt about the arranged marriage either, but we'd already decided to spend a weekend skiing together. I'd learned to ski as a child and wasn't sure if I remembered how. But if he had to teach me, that wouldn't be such a bad thing, would it? Anyway, Winter needed an ally against the frost giants. Or maybe I would look into joining NATO?

You can't date me from Boston, I texted back.

What if I came to Winter.

Do you even know how to get here?

Pretty sure there's a Lufthansa flight to Finland. From there I don't know. Reindeer? It could be like a quest. Or like a road trip except with sleighs.

I looked around me at the glass walls of the greenhouse. Inside, it was all trees and leaves and blossoms. Outside, the snow was just starting to melt. At this altitude, summer came late, even in ordinary years. Here I was, the Snow Queen—what I was born to be, at least according to my mother and Baroness Hapsenkopf. I did not feel like much of a queen. However, in the last week, I had met with members of parliament from the three major parties, the heads of various labor unions, the generals who had participated in the recent coup, the Matriarch and her council of priestesses, the director of the Central Bank, and at my insistence, a selection of ordinary citizens chosen by lottery, from university professors to plumbers and seamstresses. I had been interviewed by both major newspapers, all three state television stations, and an online journal called *WW* for Women of Winter.

I did not know if I would make a good queen, but I was starting to see what needed to be done, how to restore the economy of my country. It would take a while, but these things always did. Slowly, Winter would regain its former reputation and independence from the IMF.

All right, I texted. *If you can figure out how to get here, come find me.*

Would Kay make it to my palace of white stone veined with quartz, or get lost along the way among the snows? If he made it, would I choose him or Edrik, who was after all a prince? I didn't know, but today I was the Queen of Winter, and I had more important things to think about.

For a moment, I stood among the quince trees, whose white blossoms looked like snow on the branches and fell like snow to the ground. Outside, a dusting of snow fell from the roof, like blossoms blown by the wind. Then, I turned and walked into my palace, where my future, whatever it was, awaited me.

How to Make It Snow

First you must fall down the well.

At the bottom of the well
is the country at the bottom of the well.
That is its name, the only one it has.
You have two names, either the beautiful girl
or the kind girl, depending
on what day it is.

At the bottom of the well is a green meadow,
just like in the country you came from
but different. For one thing, the cows can speak.
They say, "Scratch our backs, scratch us
under the chin," and you do.

The meadow is filled with poppies
and cornflowers. The air is warm,
and the sun is shining.

"Thank you, beautiful girl," say the cows
and you walk on.

Across the meadow, there is a narrow path
worn by cow hooves. Follow it.

First you come to the oven.
"Take me out, take me out," cries the bread.
"I'm burning up!" You take it out,
a brown wholemeal loaf. Carry it with you
for the birds—they appear later.

Next you come to the apple tree.
"Shake us down, shake us down," cry the apples.
"We're ripe!" So you shake the branches, as though
you were dancing with them.
The apples come tumbling down.
You put three in your pocket.

Now you are at the edge of the forest
and the birds call, "Feed us, feed us!"
You ask the loaf, "May I?"

"This is what I was baked for," says the loaf.

So you scatter breadcrumbs
and the birds come, sparrows and chickadees,
robins and finches and juncos,
and a nuthatch. They perch on your arms
as you feed them. Absentmindedly,
you whistle as they do.

In the forest, a wild sow approaches.
For the first time you are afraid and step back,
but she says, "My little ones are hungry,
and I smell something sweet."
You pull the apples out of your pocket.
"May I?" you ask, and the apples reply,
"This is why we fell."

You kneel while the sow watches protectively,
feeding the apples to her three piglets,
bristle-backed, with tusks just starting to form
but still striped as though someone had marked them
with her fingers. The sow nods and says,
"You are a kind girl." Then, followed by her progeny,
she disappears into the trees.
You continue alone.

It is getting dark. You have passed through the oaks
and now it is all pines. You are walking on needles.

The light is fading when you come to the cottage.
It looks like the cottage out of a fairy tale:
peaked roof like a witch's hat, dark green trim,
small-paned windows through which firelight is flickering.
Someone is waiting for you.

You have nothing left, no bread, no apples.
So you knock.

The woman who answers is old, small,
like a doll made of cornhusks.
"You're hungry," she says,
"and tired. Come in, my dear.
The soup is almost ready."

There is a fire, and a cauldron on the fire,
and a chair by the fire, and a cat in the chair,
and you can smell the soup.

"Come on, then," says the cat, and gets up,
but only to settle again in your lap
once you sit down.

Here are the things you know about the old woman:
she milks the cows, she causes the apples to ripen,
she teaches the birds their songs, she runs her fingers
along the backs of the wild piglets
to put the stripes on them.

Here are the things she knows about you:
everything, also your name.

"What are you called, my dear?" she asks.
"The beautiful girl," you answer. "Or the kind girl."
"No," she says. "From now on, you shall be
she who makes it snow.
Or Holle, for short."

Holle: it suits you.

"Here's what I'd like you to do tomorrow morning.
Sweep the floor and dust the shelves,
wash the curtains and wind the clock,
polish the silver. And when that's done,
shake out my bedspread until the feathers
fly like snowflakes. It's time for winter.
Can you do that?"

You nod. Yes, of course.

That night you sleep under the cat,
in her attic bedroom.

The next morning, you put on an apron she left for you,
then sweep the floor and dust the shelves,
wash the curtains in a metal basin,
wind the clock and polish the silver. Finally,
you stand on the cottage steps under tall pines
and shake out the old woman's bedspread.

Snow falls and falls, until
the forest is silent.

"Well done, my dear." She's wearing a gray wool coat
and carrying a battered suitcase. "Can you do that again
tomorrow morning, and the day after tomorrow?
I need to visit my sisters, and I'm not sure
when I'll be back yet.
It takes a responsible girl, but I've heard good things
about you from the cows, the bread, the apples,
the birds, even the trees. And the cat likes you."

"I'll do my best," you say.
She kisses you on both cheeks, then rises up, up,
through the trees until she is only a speck
in the colorless sky.

You go back into the cottage.
There is a cat to scratch under the chin,

and books with stories you have never read,
and you haven't introduced yourself to the clock yet.

Besides, you like your new name.
It's the right name for a woman
who makes the snow fall.

Diamonds and Toads

This fairy tale is a metaphor.

Because it really would be just as uncomfortable
to have diamonds coming out of your mouth as toads:
one hard, sharp, like a mouthful of glass. The other
soft, squishy, making you
disgusted with yourself, because . . . toads!
Ugh. At least the diamonds are valuable,
glittering in the palm of your hand,
although their edges leave your throat aching,
your mouth sore.

The diamonds knock against your teeth.
The toads make your tongue feel coated
as though a snail had crawled across it,
leaving a trail.

Once there were two girls, sisters.
One, whose name was Tabitha,
woke up in a good mood. The sun was shining.
She did not mind the sheep
bleating in the meadow,
although some days she wished
they could be eaten by wolves
so it would be quiet, just for a moment.
Her dress was hanging in the closet,
freshly pressed (her sister had done the ironing
yesterday). Her hair was curling naturally,
rather than tangling in the brush, as usual.
So she sang as she went to the well.

There she met an old woman
who was secretly a witch. (Isn't that how
it always goes?) The woman asked for water
and Tabitha gave it to her,
drawing up the pulley
with a smile and a "Lovely day, isn't it?"
She's the one who got the diamonds.

Her sister, Dolores,
woke up the next day with a headache.
It was raining, and rainy days always did that to her.
They also made her hair frizzy.
Her only clean dress
lay crumpled in the laundry basket, still damp
because Tabitha had forgotten to hang it on the clothesline.
(We can't blame her. She was dealing
with the diamond problem, still lying down
with a hot compress on her throat.)
That morning, the breakfast porridge burned
and the cat had left a half-chewed mouse in the parlor.
Ugh. So Dolores went to the well
in a foul mood
and told the woman to draw up the water herself.
She got the toads.

I told you this tale is a metaphor.
They used the diamonds
to buy more dresses, a carpet for the parlor,
a phonograph, some sturdy shoes,
and books. Quite a lot of books.
Tabitha was able to finish her degree
in library science. Eventually
a prince proposed to Tabitha, but she didn't want
to become his main source of income, better than taxes,
which parliament wouldn't let him raise, so she told him
she wasn't interested.

It was the toads that kept the garden
free of damaging insects: cutworms, leafrollers,

loopers, hornworms, rootminers, the ubiquitous beetles
that chew through rose leaves, leaving them
looking like window panes.
Dolores grew the finest cabbages, tomatoes,
aubergines. Her orchard was the only one
not devastated by a new apple borer.
Her roses were perfection.
From their hips she made a syrup for sore throats,
for which Tabitha was grateful.
She patented it and created a thriving business.

Eventually Dolores married a gentleman
with a very large garden. She's Lady Dolores, now.
Tabitha became a librarian,
so she rarely has to talk:
she can shush without triggering the diamonds.
Still, she wears a spectacular brooch
pinned to her sweater, because after all, why not?

Here is the moral: there are circumstances
in which toads are as useful as diamonds.
Or it may be, try not to get out of bed
grumpy, especially when there are witches
around. Or always be nice to old women,
because you never know.
Or maybe Tabitha and Dolores are really
one woman, and some days what comes out of our mouths
is diamonds, and other days, toads.
Which is better? I don't know.
The moral of a fairy tale
is as difficult to figure out as what to do
about cutworms and beetles, or blackspot
on the rose leaves.

The Princess and the Frog

I threw the ball into the water.
The frog came out and followed after,
bringing me the golden ball—
which I did not want at all, at all.

Princess, he said, let me eat at your table.
I fed him as well as I was able.
Princess, let me sleep on your pillow.
He crept as close as I would allow.

He said, a witch enchanted me.
I'm not what I seem, you see,
but a prince in the form of a lowly frog,
forced to live in that wretched bog

where I found and retrieved the golden ball
you had deliberately let fall.
Why did you discard your treasure?
I said, because it gave me no pleasure.

The heavy scepter and orb of state
hurt my arms with their golden weight.
The scepter still lies within the pool,
among the weeds. I don't want to rule

this country or wage the endless war
my father started. I want more
than political and diplomatic lies.
He blinked his iridescent eyes.

Kiss me, he said. And I did, despite
my misgivings. It felt appropriate,
almost as though I could hear my fate
knocking on the castle gate.

Then he turned into a prince, and I
into a frog, instantaneously.
He took me down to the pool again,
away from the troubling world of men.

There I swim in the cool green water,
and the only things that seem to matter
are the sun as it filters into the green
or the patter of a summer rain

on the leaves of the floating water lilies.
The flashing blue of dragonflies,
the stork that is my nemesis.
Who would have thought a single kiss

could release me from the strife
attendant on a human life
and bring me to the cool green heart
of the world, where all enchantments start?

Where life is still a fairy tale,
and I'm the princess of the pool.

Conversations
with the Sea Witch

In the afternoons, they wheel her out on the balcony overlooking the sea. They place her chair by the balustrade. Once there, the queen dowager waves her hand. "Leave me," she says, in a commanding voice. Then, in the shrill tones of an old woman, "Go away, go away, damn you. I want to be alone."

They, who have been trained almost from birth to obey, leave her, bowing or curtseying as they go. After all, what harm can come to her, an old woman, a cripple? They do not call her that, of course. One does not call a queen dowager such things. But their mothers and fathers called her that long ago, when she was first found half-drowned on the sea shore—the crippled girl.

"A poor crippled girl," they whispered, incredulous, when the prince emerged from her room and told his father, "I'm going to marry her. She saved my life in the storm. She has no name—not as we have names. I'll call her Melusine."

Elsewhere in the castle, the king, her son, is issuing orders, perhaps about defending the northern borders, perhaps just about the education of the young prince, his heir. The queen is walking in the garden with her ladies-in-waiting, gathering roses. The young princess, her granddaughter, has stolen into the garden, where she is playing by the water-lily pool with her golden ball. In a moment, it will fall in. She has always been fascinated by water. She takes after her grandmother—her fingers are webbed. There are delicate membranes between each finger.

In the chapel, the former king, her husband, lies in his grand tomb of black-veined green marble. Next to it is another tomb, where she will someday lie. Now, it is empty like a promise unfulfilled. She knows it is there—she can feel it patiently waiting, and she knows it will not have to wait much longer. After all, did she not exchange five hundred years of life in the sea for one human lifetime?

Once she lies beside him, completely surrounded by stone, she will have left the sea permanently at last.

But she is not thinking of that now. She is waiting for company.

She does not have to wait long. Soon after they leave—the servants, who have lives about which she knows nothing, about whom she thinks no more than she would of the white foam on a wave—the sea witch rises.

"Greetings, princess," says the witch. That, at least, is the closest we can get in translation, for she speaks the language of the sea, which is not our language. In the air, it sounds strange and guttural, like the barking of seals. In the water, it is higher, more melodious, like the song of the sleek gray dolphins that sometimes visit our waters. It carries far.

"Greetings, witch," says the queen dowager. It is obvious, from her tone, that this is an honorific. "How goes it beneath the water?"

And then the sea witch tells her: all is well at court. Her eldest sister is a beloved queen. There have been storms along the southern coast, causing shipwrecks. Which is good—that stretch of the coast was suffering from over-fishing, and this will keep the fishermen away for a while. The whales that were trapped in the main harbor of the capital city have returned to the open sea. When Melusine became queen, it was forbidden to harm a whale, and her son continues that tradition. Her middle sister's second child has recently emerged from his father's pouch. The sea-folk, although mammalian, reproduce like sea-horses: a child, once born, is deposited in the father's pouch and emerges only to suckle its mother's breast until it can fend for itself. The sea is a dangerous place. The sea-folks' children must be strong to survive.

"And how is your throat?" asks the sea witch. "Have you tried the poultice I recommended?" It is made of seaweed, boiled down into a paste.

"Better," says the queen dowager. "But I feel death coming close, witch. Coming on human feet, soft and white and tender."

"May it not come for a few years yet," says the sea witch. She herself will likely live for another hundred years. "Who will I talk to after you are gone?"

The queen dowager laughs—the situation is, after all, ironic. And then she puts her hand to her throat, because it aches.

Two old women—that is what they are. Two old women who have lost the ones they loved, whom the world has left behind. All they have now is these conversations. Do not pity them. They get more enjoyment out of these talks than you imagine.

It was, the queen dowager thinks, a fair bargain: her voice, the voice that produced the beautiful songs of the sea-folk, like dolphins calling to one another, for a pair of human legs. Of course they were useless. A witch can split a long, gray, flexible tail into a pair of legs, pink and bare, but she cannot make them functional. What is inside them will not bear a body's weight. The crippled girl, lying on the sea shore, in love with the prince she had saved from the storm, hoping against hope that somehow she could make her way to him, perhaps by crawling higher among the rocks, knew she might die there, among the pools filled with barnacles and snails. She knew the crabs and seagulls might eat her soft white flesh. The rest of her might dry up in the sun.

Was it luck or some vestige of the sea witch's magic, or true love, which has its own gravitational power, that he was walking on the shore at exactly the right time?

As soon as he saw her, he said, "You're the girl I saw among the waves. The one who rescued me."

She tried to answer—she had lost her song, not her voice—but he could not understand what she was saying, and her voice tired quickly, trying to speak through this new medium. The sea-folk learn to understand human speech, from listening to sailors in their boats and children playing along the shore. They must guard the sea from us, so they learn about us what they can. But we, proud and ignorant, thinking there is no intelligent life but that of the air, do not learn about them, and so only a few of us speak their language. Those who do are often considered mad. They spend their lives gathering things the tide has thrown up, living as they can on the detritus of the sea.

The prince carried her to the castle, put her in the grandest of guest bedrooms, and announced to his mother and father that this was the girl he was going to marry. When asked who she was, this girl with nothing—no clothes, no voice, no name—he said she was the daughter of the sea king himself. When his father asked about her dowry, he said it was safety among the waves. If she were queen, their ships would be safe—at least from the sea-folk, who often sank ships for their cargoes of furniture and figurines, which were to them the finest of trinkets, decorating their underwater caves.

In a seafaring nation, which had made its fortune from trade with distant lands—in spices, printed fabrics, hand-painted porcelain—this dowry was judged to be better than gold or jewels. And it is a fact that the fishing boats of that country had luck with their catches once the prince married the girl he had found among the tidal pools. After their marriage, the old king abdicated in favor of his son. The county had never been so prosperous as under King Cedric and Queen Melusine.

It took a few years, working with speech therapists and vocal coaches, for her to communicate clearly with her subjects, to sound merely foreign rather than outlandish and otherworldly. When she laughed, it still startled the palace staff—it sounded so much like barking. She could never learn to walk—she did not have the internal structure for locomotion on dry land. Sometimes she missed the ease of movement under water. Often in dreams she would be swimming, and she would feel the smooth movement of her tail, the strong forward thrust through water, with pleasure. But she loved the prince, later the king, who treated her with such tenderness, carrying her himself anywhere she wished to go—trying to compensate for the loss of her watery kingdom. She loved her children, with their strange pink feet and tiny toes, kicking and waving in the air as their nappies were changed or they threw tantrums. And we all make difficult choices.

The strangest thing about life on land, she told the sea witch once they started holding these conversations, was reproduction. The monthly cycle of blood, as though she were expelling a red tide. Incubating a child herself instead of depositing it in her mate's pouch, to develop safely in that second womb, coming out only for lactation. She did not understand the concept of a wet nurse. When her children were brought to her for feedings, she laid them beside her and imagined moving through the water, with them swimming alongside, latched to her breast. That is how a child of the sea-folk feeds beneath the waves.

Eventually, she taught them to swim in the palace baths, which dated to Roman times. Her legs could not give her the thrust of her lost gray tail, but with a strong breast stroke, she could pull herself through the water and recapture, for a while, what it had been like to swim through the depths of the sea.

She still swims sometimes. And she makes lace—the most delicate, intricate lace. Her fingers have grown crooked, but this is an ancient art of the sea-folk, which they learn as children: they knot strands made of seaweed, pounded and pulled into long fibers. It is a strong thread that shimmers in sunlight. Into her lace, she weaves patterns of starfish and cuttlefish and stingray. When she is too tired to do either, she reads poetry or stares out the window—the king, her husband, made sure that her bedroom window overlooked the sea. She has had a full life. She could, if she wished, spend every moment remembering it. Her childhood in the palace of her father the sea king, swimming through rooms on whose walls grew coral and anemones, coming up to the surface only to breathe the necessary air, although the sea-folk can hold their breath for hours at a time, then diving down again into her natural element. Hunting and foraging with her sisters through algae forests, for the children of the sea-folk have the freedom of the sea from a young age. Rescuing her prince from the storm after his ship went down, dragging him back to shore on a broken spar through turbulent waves. Going to the sea witch, making the fatal bargain. The years of being a wife, mother, widow.

Once a day she is wheeled out to the balcony. The sea witch comes, rising from the waves, and they speak.

Usually, their conversation follows a familiar pattern. But on this day, the queen dowager asks a question she has never asked before. It has never, before, seemed the right time to ask. "Do you regret your decision?" she asks the sea witch, wondering if she is being rude or too personal. But surely between old friends? After all this time, they must consider themselves that.

The sea witch is silent for a moment, then shakes her head. "No, at least I tried. You were not the only one, you know. I traded for your voice, the hair of another maiden, the soft gray skin of yet another. He would not love me, no matter how I tried to please him. He loved no one but himself."

He lived in the deepest, darkest abyss in those parts, an underwater crevasse that seemed to descend to the center of the earth. None of the sea-folk knew how old he was. Four hundred years? Six hundred? Older yet? He had filled himself with the magic of those dark spaces, and did not seem to age.

"He taught me so much," says the sea witch. "From him, I learned a magic that allowed me to stay under water for days at a time. A magic that raised the waves and created storms. The magic that took your voice. For years, I studied spells and potions under his tutelage. But when I told him that I loved him, he called me a silly guppy, no wiser than an infant, and told me to go away, that I was interrupting his studies. I did not go away—I moved to the edge of the crevasse in which he lived, and there I stayed, living in the cavern in which you found me. I hoped that if he saw my devotion, he would come to love me in time. But it merely irritated him.

"He cared only for knowledge—only for discovering the secrets of that dark abyss and the power it would give him. At first he would go to the surface periodically. But after he drove me out, he began to stay beneath the water for weeks at a time. He told me he no longer needed to breath air. His eyes grew larger, his once-muscular body thinner. He developed a permanent look of hunger. I do not think he ate, except when krill or small shrimp floated by and he could catch them without interrupting his studies. He became hunched, as though curled up on himself. I did not care. I had not loved him for his beauty, which was considerable, but for his intellect, his desire for knowledge. I thought he might admire those things in me as well, so after my attempts to charm him failed, I studied the darkest of arts, the most potent of potions.

"One day, I perfected a spell that was beyond even his power. It was one he had attempted many times himself: a way of turning our tails into the tentacles of a squid, with the squid's ability to darken the water with its ink. I cast it, triumphant, knowing that he must love me now, or if not love, then at least respect me. At last, feeling the reverberations of that spell in the water, he came to my cavern.

"I thought he would be pleased that I had discovered this secret—that he would praise me and want to learn it from me. But no—he hurled himself at me with the full thrust of his tail and struck me across the face. Then, with his hands, he attempted to strangle me. But you see, I had eight new tentacles that I had not yet learned to control . . ."

The sea witch pauses for a moment, then says, "I tore him limb from limb. I could not even see—the water was dark with my ink. When it cleared, there were pieces of him scattered among the coral. The small fish were already nibbling at his flesh."

Then they are both silent, the queen dowager in her wheeled chair on the balcony, the sea witch floating among the waves, her body half out of water, a woman above, an octopus below.

* * *

What are we left with in the end, but old women telling stories? The first old women who told stories were the Fates. What else could they do, sitting in their chairs all day, spinning, measuring, and cutting the threads of our lives? Each thread was also a story, and as they spun it, they told it. They are telling our stories still.

Once upon a time, says Clotho as she spins the thread on her spindle. There was a king with three sons, the youngest of whom was called Dumbling, or the prettiest girl you have ever seen who was born with the feathers of a swan, or a queen who could not bear a child until a white snake told her that she was pregnant. And then, says Lachesis, the lass lived happily with her bear husband until she wanted to see what he looked like at night, or the prince found a castle in the forest inhabited entirely by cats, or the cook was so hungry that she took a spoonful of soup and all the sudden she could understand the language of animals. Finally, says Atropos, the loyal servant chopped off the brown bull's head and there stood the prince he had been searching for, or the maid spun linen so fine that it could fit through the eye of a needle so the Tsar took her back to his palace, or the false princess was put in a barrel filled with nails drawn by two white horses, and did she regret her treachery! They lived happily ever after, or not, and they are feasting still unless they have died in the interval. Every story has a beginning, middle, and end. After that end, there are only old women sitting together in the sunshine.

"And were you happy?" asks the sea witch.

"Very happy," says the queen dowager. "I'm still happy, even when I lie awake at night in a bed that is too large for one shrunken old woman, remembering tenderness that will never come again. Even when I know that soon my body will lie in a dry, dark place. My granddaughter, the youngest, Eglantine—I think someday she will come find you and ask to return to the sea. When she does, I hope you will give her my tail."

She pauses a moment. "And were you happy?" she asks the sea witch, for everyone deserves a little happiness in life, even witches.

The sea witch thinks for a moment. "No, I cannot say that I was. But I learned a great deal. No one in the sea, or perhaps even on land, has the knowledge I do. If I wished to, I could send a storm to destroy all the ships in this harbor, like a boy breaking sticks. Of course I would not do that, out of courtesy to you . . ." She bows to the queen dowager, who bows in return. "But I could, and that is something. Knowledge and power—those count for something when one is old."

"As do the memory of loving and being loved," says the queen dowager.

And then they are silent for a while, enjoying the sunshine and the lapping of waves.

"Well, until tomorrow," says the sea witch, finally. She knows the queen dowager's attendants will be coming soon.

"Of course," says the queen dowager.

The thread is spun, measured, and snipped, whether it be gold or hemp or sea silk. And afterward, the old women sit in the sunshine.

The Nightingale and the Rose

Here is the story:

There was a nightingale.
She looked like nothing at all,
a small brown bird
perched in the rose bushes.
You would scarcely have seen her
unless you were looking carefully.

The roses were still blooming
although it was late summer:
they were hybrid perpetuals, bred
from the old French roses
crossed with roses from China
brought back by sailors and diplomats,
in cargoes with blue porcelain
and embroidered silk.

The nightingale did not know this:
she had not migrated so far.

What she knew was her nest in the thicket
by the orchard, with two eggs in it the size
of your thumbnail, speckled brown.

What she knew was the professor's garden:
the elm tree, the fountain in which she bathed,
shaking her feathers. The sundial
that told the time and all the local gossip.

The green lizards sunbathing on the wall,
the tennis lawn, the roses in clipped rows,
already losing their petals,
yellow and pink, pink striped red,
apricot, and cream with a yellow heart.
She knew they cost a great deal, for the professor
had said so, walking in the garden
with the university chancellor,
and the lizards had repeated it.

She knew the student who lived with the professor
in a rented room and sometimes left his books
on the garden bench. She knew he was studying
something called metaphysics.

She knew the professor's daughter,
who walked in the garden and often sang to herself
while cutting flowers—not quite as well
as a nightingale, but one must make allowances.
Anyway, the nightingale thought she was beautiful,
with rich brown hair. But the butterflies
thought she was ugly, so large and human,
always taking away the flowers
so they could be displayed in vases behind glass windows,
and what was the use of that? They were convinced
the flowers belonged to them. After all,
they were the ones who depended on the nectar
for food. They were socialists.

One day as she sat in her nest, the nightingale heard
the student complaining to the lizards, or perhaps to the wall:
She promised to dance with me if I brought her a red rose
to match her dress, but there are no red roses,
only pink streaked with red, or red on the yellow petals.
The lizards scurried along the wall. They did not care
about the student's relationship problems.

But the nightingale was a romantic.
I shall find him a red rose, she thought.

The student was right: there were no red roses,
not anywhere in the professor's garden.
Why do you want a red rose? asked the Boule de Neige.
It was the most beautiful rose in the garden, and knew it.
Its buds were red, but opened into white globes
of fragrance. A white rose means innocence,
a white rose means *I am pure.*

Because the professor's daughter wants it, said the nightingale.
And red roses mean love. That's what she truly wants: proof
that the student loves her. And then perhaps
she will permit herself to love him back. Can you not turn
your petals red? For love
is the best thing in the world. Or what she had seen
of the world, from Denmark to the coast of Africa.
She had migrated once already.

Look how the sun loves the waterdrops
that splash from the fountain,
how the wind loves the top of the elm tree,
how the lizards love their wall. That is how
the student loves the professor's daughter,
I'm sure of it.

There is only one way to turn a white rose red,
said the Boule de Neige. And it is so terrible
that I do not want to mention it.

Tell me, said the nightingale.
I'm not afraid.

You see that rose? My most beautiful rose
at the end of an arching cane. If you perch
on that cane and put your breast against the thorn,
then press on it, so it drinks of your heart's blood,
and you sing—remember that you must sing—
slowly the rose will turn red.

The nightingale chirped
and flitted about in her agitation.
But my heart's blood—will I not die?
She thought of her eggs, her precious eggs,
speckled brown, the size of your thumbnail.
She loved her eggs, as much as the student
loved metaphysics. They had been laid in June,
for she had mated late. In a few days
they would hatch.

That I can't tell you, said the Boule de Neige.
Very likely, but one must take risks for love,
or so I have heard.

I don't know, I don't know, said the nightingale.
Let me return this evening. I must consider
all the options.

The rest of that day, she sat on her eggs.
What if she never came back, and they did not hatch?
What if they hatched and she was not there
when her children called for her? Who would teach them to fly?
It was the male nightingales, after all, who sang at night,
as her mate had sung to her before an owl
had made a meal of him. Who was she
to do this?

And yet she could already imagine
the red rose, the most beautiful of all roses,
that her song would produce.
She felt this task had been given to her.
In all the garden, only she
could sing a red rose into being.

That evening, as the moon climbed the sky,
she left her nest in the thicket and flew to the rose bushes.
She perched on the arching cane with the most beautiful rose
on it, white as snow. I'm ready, she said.
All right, said the Boule de Neige. We shall do this together.

She put her breast on the thorn so it pierced deeply
and sang. She sang all the songs she had learned
since she had hatched from an egg—
songs of courtship, songs of warning, songs about rain,
songs that meant *The cat is coming.*

The lizards said, what is that racket? But the sundial
liked it, and the fountain accompanied her as well as it could,
and the other rose bushes, who knew what was happening,
listened intently: the Variegata de Bologna,
the Reine des Violettes, the Souvenir de la Malmaison,
who claimed descent from Empress Josephine herself.
Even the daisies in the tennis lawn understood
and blushed to be witnessing an event so important.

The student up in his garret bedroom
said, How prettily the nightingale is singing!
as he leafed through his Kant and Hegel.

Only the professor's daughter did not hear it,
for she was practicing at the pianoforte
and anyway the French doors were closed.

All night long the nightingale sang,
and by morning the rose was as red as her heart's blood,
as red as the velvet mantle of a king,
or a ruby worn by an American heiress.
Even the dawn was astonished
and touched it delicately.

But what about the nightingale? She lay
on the rich soil of the rose bed,
her small heart barely beating. Had it been worth it?
She thought it had, she was almost certain.
For during that long night it had come to her
that the rose, despite being beautiful, was beside the point.
For the point—and here she gasped, her beak open
to take a final breath—was the song, and becoming the song.

Before breakfast, the student walked into the garden.
A red rose! And the most magnificent one
he had ever seen. Surely she would dance with him now
at the party the professor was throwing that evening
for his department. There would be a waltz, he was sure of it.
He would hold her tightly around the waist, and she would dance
with him, and maybe kiss him in the conservatory.

Look, he said, showing it to her
over toast and marmalade in the breakfast room.
It will match your dress perfectly.
Oh, she said. But I'm not wearing that dress anymore.

Where had he found the rose? She had asked for a red one
because there were none in the garden. Tonight, she was planning
to slip away during the mazurka, when no one would notice,
and elope with her cousin, whom she had loved since they were children
spending summers together at their grandparents' house in Funen.
Her father had quarreled with his father and forbidden her
to see him, so they had been meeting in secret.
She wore his engagement ring on a chain under her bodice.
Tomorrow they would be married. They were risking
everything—the anger of their fathers, disinheritance.
But at least they would be together.
She did not want the student searching for her at the party,
preventing her escape. Why could he not have fallen
in love with someone else, like the kitchen maid?

Later the student, despondent,
on his way to the university, discovered
that he had inadvertently tucked the rose into his satchel,
not knowing what else to do with it.
With an oath he flung it into the street,
where a cartwheel ran over it
and a horse's hooves trampled it
into the mud. Love is a fool's game,
he thought. Better stick
with what can be learned in books.

That night, after the party was over,
the professor snoring in his nightcap, the student
sprawled on his bed, still in his clothes
(he would have a hangover the next morning),
the professor's daughter in a coach rolling toward Copenhagen,
her head on her cousin's shoulder, the marriage license
tucked safely in his waistcoat pocket, only the kitchen maid
still awake, washing the last of the coffee cups,

Mother Night came walking down the street.
The pear and quince trees in the orchard bowed,
as did the elm. The fountain spit its waters
as hard and high as it could so the drops would sparkle
like fireworks under the moon. The daisies
grew pale—they were very young. The rose bushes,
who were well-bred, bent their canes gracefully.
Even the lizards, despite being diurnal, blinked their eyes
in the moonlight. And the old house itself, which had stood
since before the Reformation, said to her,
Lady, I am not worthy
of this honor.

She smiled and said, I believe you have something here
that was made for me? Ah, yes.
She stooped in the street, on which the mud had dried,
and picked up the rose, crushed, its petals scattered.
then put it into her dark hair, fastening it
with a jeweled pin. There, it blossomed
and its fragrance filled the garden. In that house
all the sleepers, from the professor to the cook,
would have strange dreams.

She stroked the timbers of the house, which creaked with pleasure,
then scratched the lizards under their chins. To the roses,
she nodded, as great ladies nod to each other,
and they nodded back, knowingly. She smiled
at the daisies, who immediately closed up with shyness.
Finally, she lifted the nightingale, lying
stiff and lifeless, then breathed on her, long and slow.

The nightingale gasped and fluttered. When she saw
the face bent over her,
she hid her head beneath her wing.

Such humility, said Mother Night. And in a great artist.
Would you like to sing in my garden at the end of the world?
The nightingale, not knowing what to say,
gave one small trill, but that was enough.

Pardon me, said Mother Night to the wall,
reaching into the thicket and lifting the nightingale's nest,
then putting the nightingale on her speckled eggs. Carrying
the nest in the palm of her hand, she proceeded up the street,
for she had a great deal to do before sunrise.

In Paris she picked up a poet
who had died that day of meningitis
in a hotel room, after being released from prison.
She put him into her pocket, already filled
with all the oddments she had collected that night.
Still carrying the nightingale's nest,
she walked to the end of the world, to her house
of many rooms, some large as the sky,
some small as a mouse hole,
where everything precious is preserved.

If you ever find it—it's not on any map
and you can only go there by invitation—
sit in the garden, just at twilight,
and hear the nightingales. There are three of them.
They are said to be very fine.

Mirror, Mirror

Each morning, standing barefoot on cold tiles,
I ask you, not who is the fairest in the land—
I'm neither that vain nor ambitious.

But am I as fair as I was
yesterday, or the day before yesterday,
all the yesterdays on which I was younger
than I am today. Those lines that Mother Time,
the indefatigable spider,
is spinning beneath my eyes—have they spread overnight?
Perhaps I should stop smiling so frequently.

Perhaps I should stop frowning, avoid the sun—
already it has painted a few brown spots
on my cheeks and forehead. Or sleep for a hundred years,
which is as effective, they say, as a facelift.

Each morning you say, yes, you are older now.
There are white hairs on either side of your forehead,
looking as though they had been touched by Frost,
whose fingers leave precisely such fine streaks
over the meadow grasses, the windowpanes.
Soon, you will become a winter landscape
crossed by tracks where hare and deer have passed
on their way into the darkness of the forest.
Soon, you will sprout mushrooms.

Wake up, wake up! you say.
You will sleep all too soon—now is the time
to live as though you were going to live forever,

as though winter never comes
and all the fairy tales
were true.

Acknowledgments

I don't remember when I started reading fairy tales, although I still have my first fairy tale books: *Kis Gyermekek Nagy Mesekönyve*, *Grimm Legszebb Meséi*, and Elek Benedek's *Ezüst Mesekönyv*, whose strange, beautiful illustrations kept me up at night. These books exposed me to a world beyond my grandparents' apartment in Budapest, where I spent the earliest years of my life. Later, they helped me adjust to life in new cities: Milan, Brussels, and finally Washington, D.C., where I grew up. Although I graduated to children's stories like *Alice in Wonderland* and *The Wizard of Oz*, and then adult stories of fantasy and magical realism, fairy tales never left me. They are some of the most powerful narratives human beings have produced, about what we most want (beauty, home, bread) and fear (darkness, abandonment, being devoured), which is why they keep being retold and reconfigured. I returned to them as an adult, when I began doing some of that reconfiguring myself. Now I teach fairy tales to university students, who often haven't read the older versions by Basile, Perrault, and the Grimms. Hopefully, they come out of the class appreciating the power and complexity of these old tales. It is a privilege to have read them when I was young, and to participate in the long tradition of reimagining them for a new era.

There are so many people without whom the stories and poems in this book would not have been written or published. I would like to thank the following editors not only for buying them, but also for the insightful comments that made my writing better than I could have made it on my own: Shawna McCarthy ("The Rose in Twelve Petals"), Karen Meisner ("Sleeping with Bears"), Paula Guran ("Blanchefleur"), Navah Wolfe and Dominik Parisien ("The Other Thea"), Ellen Datlow ("Red as Blood and White as Bone"), Terri Windling ("The Bear's Daughter" and "What Her Mother Said"), Mike and Anita Allen ("The Bear's Wife"), and Julia Rios ("Rose

Child" and "Seven Shoes"). I would doubly like to thank Mike and Anita for making this book possible—it would not exist without their editorial guidance and the wonderful work of Mythic Delirium Books. My heartfelt thanks to Jane Yolen for her magnificent introduction—her writing has influenced and uplifted me for years, and it is a privilege to have her words at the beginning of this book. A second heartfelt thanks goes to Ruth Sanderson for her magical illustration. I can't imagine a more beautiful and fitting image for the cover. I'm very lucky to be part of a community of fairy-tale writers and scholars who have helped me understand and reinterpret these old stories: thank you to Maria Tatar, Cristina Bacchilega, Christie Williams, Claudia Schwabe, Veronica Schanoes, and Helen Pilinovsky for all they have taught me about fairy tales. I would also like to thank all the students who have taken my classes on fairy tales over the years—they have taught me so much more than I have taught them. And finally, I would like to thank my daughter Ophelia, who is a constant source of joy and inspiration—a fairy tale come true.

About the Author

Theodora Goss is the World Fantasy and Locus Award-winning author of the short story collection *In the Forest of Forgetting* (2006); *Interfictions* (2007), a short story anthology coedited with Delia Sherman; *Voices from Fairyland* (2008), a poetry anthology with critical essays and a selection of her own poems; *The Thorn and the Blossom* (2012), a novella in a two-sided accordion format; the poetry collection *Songs for Ophelia* (2014); debut novel *The Strange Case of the Alchemist's Daughter* (2017), and sequel *European Travel for the Monstrous Gentlewoman* (2018). She has been a finalist for the Nebula, Crawford, Seiun, and Mythopoeic Awards, as well as on the Tiptree Award Honor List. Her work has been translated into twelve languages. She teaches literature and writing at Boston University and in the Stonecoast MFA Program. Learn more at theodoragoss.com.